D0321187

Items should be returned on or before the last date
shown below. Items not already requested by other
borrowers may be renewed in person, in writing or by
telephone. To renew, please quote the number on the
barcode label. To renew online a PIN is required.
This can be requested at your local library.
Renew online @ **www.dublincitypubliclibraries.ie**
Fines charged for overdue items will include postage
incurred in recovery. Damage to or loss of items will
be charged to the borrower.

Leabharlanna Poiblí Chathair Bhaile Átha Cliath
Dublin City Public Libraries

Dublin City
Baile Átha Cliath

Brainse Mheal Ráthluirc
Charleville Mall Branch
Tel 8749619

Date Due	Date Due	Date Due
22. JUL. 06		
20. JUL. 10	04. JUN 13.	
30. 03. 12.	0 8 APR 2022	
01. NOV 12		
24/6/15		

A MOTHER'S NIGHTMARE

my fight to get my children back

LOUISE MASON

BLACKSTAFF PRESS

BELFAST

First published in 2009 by
Blackstaff Press
4c Heron Wharf, Sydenham Business Park
Belfast BT3 9LE

© Louise Mason and Felicity McCall, 2009
All rights reserved

Louise Mason and Felicity McCall have asserted their rights under
the Copyright, Designs and Patents Act 1988
to be identified as the authors of this work.

Typeset by CJWT Solutions, St Helens, England

Printed in England by Cox and Wyman

A CIP catalogue record for this book is available
from the British Library

ISBN 978-0-85640-830-4

www.blackstaffpress.com

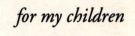

for my children

CONTENTS

Preface

In compliance with legal requirements and to protect the identity of two of my youngest children, I have referred to them throughout this book as J and K. A ruling from the High Court permits that only their ages – seven and five respectively in 2008 – should be made known, not their sex, which has caused some difficulties in the text. Although not strictly grammatically correct, I have at times used the pronoun 'their' rather than 'his' or 'her'. The seven- and five-year-olds' father is referred to as X, as specified in the same ruling. For the purposes of this book, I've called my older children Jaz, Nina, Ayshea and Jake, and called my youngest child Chloe. Similarly, I've called a former friend and her brother Janice and Peter. I've replaced all the doctors' names with initials given that much of their evidence was in the context of private proceedings.

It feels strange to me, not using my children's real names, but I hope readers will understand the reasons for this.

The Long Journey

On 19 November 2004, I walked free from Londonderry Crown Court in Northern Ireland after being acquitted of causing grievous bodily harm to my four-week-old baby in 2002. The trial had lasted two weeks, the most nerve-wracking period of my life, and I'll never forget the moment when the jury filed back into the courtroom to return their verdict. As the foreperson said the words 'not guilty', one woman juror wept openly. I clasped my hands and turned to thank the jury, and to thank God, and Saint Teresa, whose prayer card I'd carried with me throughout.

For the two hard years that it had taken for my case to come to trial, I had tried to stay strong, knowing I was innocent. Now the suppressed tension, and sheer exhaustion, hit home and I felt as though I was going to collapse.

The verdict marked the end of a long legal struggle to prove my innocence. During that time, I had been

Leabharlanna Poibli Chathair Bhaile Átha Cliath

Dublin City Public Libraries

separated from my children – the Foyle Health and Social Services Trust had taken the youngest two into care as soon as the allegations against me were made. Unknown to the jurors, to most of the people who had crowded the public gallery during the trial, and to the journalists who had reported on it so assiduously from the press bench, my struggle to win back care and custody of my children was far from over. For also unknown to them, and kept undisclosed in the interests of a fair trial, was the fact that a Family Court, held behind closed doors, without a jury, away from public and media attention, had already concluded that I had injured my baby and that my children should not be returned to my care. The Trust was now moving to have the children adopted.

My solicitor, Carmel McGilloway, had explained to me that it was not expected that the Trust would force the adoption issue until the criminal proceedings had been disposed of. My legal team made no secret of the fact that, at the time, there was no precedent for stopping a freeing order for adoption. Such an order had always been successful. I'd run out of the consulting room in panic and despair when they'd told me; now I had to face grim reality. My children were, in effect, only weeks away from being lost to me until their eighteenth birthdays, if not forever. As it was, I was allowed to see them for just an hour and a half each month. These visits were supervised by social services staff and held in the austere and unwelcoming surroundings of Shantallow Health Centre; far from the loving, happy, comfortable family home I'd been creating for us.

The next day's headlines would start the process of clearing my name. I tried to cling to the fervent belief, expressed by the man who ran the prayer group I'd been attending, that everything would be all right.

Moving to Ireland

It was all a far cry from 21 October 2001 – the day that I'd landed at Belfast International Airport with two of my children, Ayshea and J, a few suitcases and a heart full of hope, to begin the seventy-mile journey to the city of Derry. There, I planned to make a fresh start for my whole family and me. I wanted so much to build a new life away from the domestic upheaval of the past few years, away from my ex-husband, Sol. All I ever wanted was to have my five children gathered under one roof, and to live a peaceful, contented life.

It wasn't a complete step into the unknown. I'd already been to Derry several times over the summer of that year. My partner, X, was from Derry. We'd met in 1999 when he was working in my home town of Northampton and staying with his uncle and aunt. Although we had become estranged, I'd gone to Derry over the summer to try and patch things up with him and to take our four-month-old, J, to meet the Irish grandmother, and huge extended family, for the first time. They'd adored the little one, and made no secret of the fact they hoped X and I could rekindle our troubled relationship. I knew this would mean moving to Derry, where he intended to stay.

It was a big decision. As well as baby J, I had four children in Northampton from two previous relationships. Their fathers – Sol and my former fiancé, Trevor – both lived in Northampton. But I still had very strong feelings for X, and my other children had got on well with him and missed him. All I had to do now, I convinced myself, was to find a comfortable family house and good schools in Derry, and make the arrangements for the rest of the family to join me once the school term ended. My mum and dad, Pauline and Stanley, who had played a big part in the children's upbringing, were looking after the eldest two, Jaz and Nina, who had decided to stay in Northampton for now. The third, Ayshea, who was almost eleven, had decided to come with me. Trevor and I have joint custody of my fourth child, Jake, and we had mutually agreed that he would spend term-time with his father in Northampton and the school holidays with me. We'd travel to England once a month to spend the weekend with him. I concentrated on everything that looked positive about my planned move.

The first thing that had struck me about Derry in the summer was that it was so green. Every housing development had its grassy areas and parks. The countryside was only minutes away. The beaches and coastline were spectacularly beautiful. The people I'd met had been friendly and welcoming. I'd had good reports of the education system. Attending Mass here was still very much part of family life, while in England it was a bit unusual. Most of my children's friends didn't go to a place of worship. My faith has sustained me through the crises in my life and I wanted to bring up my children to have a sense of spirituality. Derry had a lot to offer a large, growing family.

If that sounds like a huge step to take, on my own, I should explain that I've always been very independent and strong-minded. Born in Northampton in 1969, I was the youngest of three and grew up very much on my own. Dad was a plasterer by trade. Mum ran her own cleaning business, which involved working long hours. My brother, Stephen, is eleven years older than me, and my sister, Deborah, seven years older, so they'd grown up and left home before I reached my teens. We were surrounded by extended family; Mum was very close to her own mother, and aunts, uncles and cousins all lived within a few streets; but I tended to be a bit of a loner, doing my own thing. My lasting memory of those years is of coming home from school to a spotless house – that was always empty. I loved children and earned money babysitting for family and neighbours as soon as I was old enough. I always wanted a big family of my own. My parents weren't too concerned about what I did; they were very relaxed about letting me make all my own decisions from a remarkably young age. They never got involved. I won't sit back when my children are making decisions that will change their lives.

I was a feisty girl and disliked school. I left as soon as I could, at fifteen. I didn't even go back to sit my exams, though I know now, from studying nursing as a mature student, that I would have been capable of achieving reasonably good grades. By the time I left school, I'd also met my first steady boyfriend, Chris. He was twenty-six and a local taxi driver who used to run me home when I was babysitting. Mum didn't baulk at the big age difference. He was kind and reliable, so she was quite happy when I moved out to live in a flat with him, even though I was still only fifteen. I got a job in a local restaurant to pay my way.

When I think back on our relationship, maybe I was looking for a sense of security. I suppose Chris represented something of a father figure to me. At a time when my friends were running to clubs and discos, I was keeping house, working shifts and babysitting. But I was content; Chris was more than kind to me. When I did move on – shortly before my seventeenth birthday, to share a bedsit with an old school friend, Susan – Chris and I remained friends and we kept in touch until he died, when he was still young, of cancer. I will always remember how good he was to me.

When I was nineteen, I met Sol through mutual friends. Another older man. About eight years older than me, Sol was a Libyan who had come to England to study when he was eighteen and had stayed. He was dark and handsome, with a well-paid engineering position and he was training for further qualifications. Although he was born a Muslim, Sol was very westernised and enjoyed drinking and socialising, often a bit too much.

A few months after we met I was shocked to discover I was pregnant. I had been taking the contraceptive pill. In spite of the surprise, it never crossed my mind to do anything other than keep the baby. I moved back in with my parents, who were very supportive. Every week Mum would buy something for the baby – a cot, a chair, a duvet, tiny outfits. My sister Deborah came with me to my first scan; I was thrilled to see the little miracle growing within me. I loved that little baby straightaway.

I had a happy, healthy pregnancy. Although I was young, I never felt I was losing out on anything by becoming a parent. I looked forward to the baby's arrival. Mum liked Sol and welcomed him into our family home. His family in Libya was very wealthy, and he was generous to my parents. If he had any reservations about the pregnancy, they disappeared on that day in April 1989 when he joined Mum and me in the postnatal ward and held his son for the first time. He made no secret of his delight that we'd had a little boy. We called him Jaz. He told me the news had been greeted ecstatically in Libya.

In September we were married by a mullah at a short, informal wedding ceremony attended by a small group of Sol's Muslim friends. The service was held in a house belonging to a friend of Sol's and we didn't even dress up for the occasion. Divorce is not recognised in the Muslim faith, so in that respect I'm still married to him. Shortly after, we had a small, civil marriage ceremony in the local registry office. Again, only a few friends came as witnesses.

Jaz was a very easy baby, a good feeder and sleeper who was soon in a routine. He had a lovely, placid nature, which was just as well, as within a few months, I was pregnant again.

Although I was pleased about being pregnant, I was worried that Sol and I were drifting apart. Cracks in our marriage began to appear. I felt that Sol had a bit of a casual attitude to relationships. He liked women. I suspected he'd had at least one affair already. Maybe I was too possessive, or too jealous, or pregnancy made me over-sensitive, but he had never denied that on one occasion my suspicions were correct. When I confronted him, he admitted to me that he was seeing another woman – and that she was pregnant and due to give birth about the same time as I was. I was very, very upset and we fought about it constantly. From then on we went from blazing row to passionate reconciliation, over and over again. As I said, when I was younger I had a very strong personality and I wasn't gong to sit back meekly and put up with this. I issued Sol with an ultimatum and he stayed. I later found out that the other girl terminated her pregnancy. Once Sol had made the decision to stay in the marriage, things began to improve. He and I were close during the last few months of my pregnancy, and

Nina was born, safe and well, almost exactly a year after her brother.

Four months after Nina was born, Sol and I and our two children moved into our own home in Kingsthorpe, not far from my parents. Sol had been living with me at my mum and dad's house for a few months before that, but it was great to have our own little nest and I loved being a full-time mum. We were happy and the kids were thriving. In April of the following year, I discovered that I was pregnant again and in December 1991, Ayshea arrived. She reminded me very much of Jaz as an infant – sweet-natured and placid. It was Nina who showed a strong, independent streak. Even when she was a toddler, she was more forceful than her siblings.

So by the time I was in my early twenties, I had three little ones under school age. Sol was not one to participate in day-to-day childcare or housework. Mum, on the other hand, was brilliant and got very involved in her grandchildren's daily routine – much more so than she had been with me when I was young. She had scaled down her own work and was supportive of me getting a job outside the home.

Soon we were in a position, with the council's help, to rent a lovely, three-storey terrace. I registered Jaz and Nina for places at the local school. I went looking for work in the catering and hospitality trade, the only one I knew, and began by doing shifts and weekend work in a local bar-cum-restaurant. It was great to be back at work and have some financial independence.

But my marriage was falling apart. The break-ups and make-ups had grown closer and closer together and were increasingly draining. It was not the right atmosphere in which to bring up children. Sol's a social person and enjoyed his nightlife. He wasn't one to sit at home at night, the direct opposite to me. He was never more than a social drinker, but I'm not keen on alcohol and the pub and club scene. Sol saw no reason to change. He enjoyed it. I also suspected Sol was seeing other women, although nothing was ever proven.

After one confrontation too many, he moved out. For his own reasons, he felt it was best to opt for a clean, complete break. The children were still small and for a number of years he had no contact with them. He also stopped providing any financial support. I never applied for a maintenance order – which would have meant access – so in a way I suppose I chose a clean break too.

I increased my working hours to help make ends meet. Mum very kindly agreed to look after the children for longer. I loved the job. By now I'd been asked to run the restaurant on a daily basis. I found I'd a natural talent for organisation and a gift for keeping things clean and orderly, skills that must have been passed on to me by my mother. At that age I was more easy-going with new people and liked talking to the customers. I was quite confident, for a time, in my early twenties, before my troubles knocked it out of me.

Although I enjoyed my work, I loved spending time with the kids, too. We would read stories, draw pictures, go out to the park or swimming pool. Even though we didn't have much, I did all I could to make sure the kids had the best of everything. I'd set up a club card arrangement at a local clothes shop, then carefully chose the children's outfits, paying them off at an agreed amount each week. I discovered, to my amusement, that they were known locally as 'The Catalogue Kids' because their dark hair, lustrous dark eyes and olive skin made them look like three little models.

As I'm not one for pubs or clubs, my 'entertainment', from a young age, has always been found through work, or my children. I loved taking them out for the day and wished there were more parks and green spaces near us. Just cuddling up together on the sofa with a video was a treat. Life was a busy round of cooking, cleaning, washing, ironing and work, but I loved my kids and they loved me and that made up for any tiredness or sacrifice, many times over.

I was twenty-five, had three young children and was still running the restaurant when I met Trevor. He was a couple of years younger than me and worked in information technology. He was a regular at my place of work and we'd often stand chatting to each other. When we began going out together, it was clear he loved children and most of our 'dates' were spent with my three kids. Trevor fitted in very naturally and was endlessly patient and involved with their world in a way their father had never been.

Again, my mum liked him and encouraged the relationship. She could see he made us all happy. Gradually, I fell in love. It was a completely different experience – gentle and contented. A year later, we got engaged and planned to marry a few years after that. Trevor had been keen to start a family as soon as I would agree, and when I discovered I was pregnant in November 1996, we were both delighted. Jake was very much a planned baby.

In retrospect, I think it was from Jake's birth that things started to go wrong between us. Trevor wanted to be at the birth, so I agreed. It was a straightforward delivery, but obviously came as a shock to him. He admitted afterwards that he found it gory and distressing. He said it changed the way he felt about me and I realised he wasn't sexually attracted to me any more. We settled into a relationship in which we were more like friends than lovers. I knew it wasn't ideal – we were only in our twenties, after all – but I loved Trevor, and I loved the fact that he was such a good father. It was such a contrast to Sol. Trevor adored his son and spent as much time as he could with him. I had three other little ones to care for – they doted on their new little brother, but needed my love and attention as much as before.

Jake developed a very close bond with Trevor, one that has become stronger as the years go by. Looking back, I can see that a lot of the time Trevor was with Jake while I was with Jaz, Nina and Ayshea, who were now eight, seven and six. I was spending time on paired reading, homework, arts and crafts, while Trevor was changing nappies and making feeds.

On the surface, family life went on as before, and we all worked well together as a team. But by the time Jake was a year old, I realised with growing dread that the man I loved no longer felt the same way about me. Our plan to get married in a couple of years had been put on hold. I didn't force the issue; I was too scared. I had thought Trevor and I would be together forever. There were no rows. He's not that sort of man. But I knew there was a distance between us and I couldn't do anything about it. We had a kind, polite friendship and we respected each other and treated each other well. But there was nothing more. The older children and I were like one little family and Trevor and Jake were another friendly family under the same roof. Trevor had always wanted a child more than anything and he was so happy that I had given him Jake. But after Jake was born, I think all his love and attention was poured into the baby. He didn't need me any more. Jake was enough.

One night, just after Christmas 1998, we were sitting together watching *Cold Feet* on television. The children were tucked up in bed, fast asleep. I didn't want to raise the issue of our relationship because I knew the answer already. But I also knew we couldn't go on like this. We got talking about the characters' relationships on television. Then I asked about ours. Taking courage, I said to Trevor: 'You don't love me any more.' Quietly, almost embarrassedly, he agreed. 'I don't. I'm sorry.'

True to the nature of our relationship, we did not row. Trevor moved out to a house nearby and we agreed to joint custody of Jake. Jake would spend weekends and Wednesday nights with Trevor and he would be with us the rest of the time. I knew Trevor was a very loving, capable father and felt this was a good arrangement for Jake.

I was very down for quite a while. Trevor hadn't loved me for a long time but I missed him.

Now it was just me and the children. Jaz, Nina and Ayshea were settled in school by now and, if I was working, Mum would take care of them after classes and at weekends. It was clear that Jaz was bright, Nina was full of energy and very strong-minded, which occasionally got her into trouble, and Ayshea was an easy-going little girl who was popular and made friends easily. Jake was also settled in a small nursery and happily split his time between me and Trevor.

Everything was going well until Ayshea's accident. I don't know whether she hit something on the road, or lost her balance, but she toppled off her bike and fell heavily on the ground. Blood poured from her head. She screamed in pain. Running to her, I shouted for someone to call an ambulance. Sitting in the back with my little daughter on the way to hospital, I insisted that her father should be contacted. We hadn't seen him for almost two years, but he needed to know what had happened. Gradually Ayshea pulled through. She had fractured her skull but mercifully went on to make a full recovery.

Following the accident, Sol was now back in the children's lives, though for a long time it wasn't on any regular basis, which was upsetting for them.

With the children getting older – they were ten, nine, eight and two in 1999 – I decided I wanted a career, not just a job. I knew I was capable of doing more with my life. The children were growing up, I had a bit more free time, and it would give us financial security. I decided it was time to start studying and get some formal qualifications. I'd told Jake's health visitor that I was interested in nursing, perhaps midwifery. She was very supportive and together we tracked down a five-year, part-time course that was ideal for someone like me with no academic qualifications. If it went well, I'd be fully qualified by the time Jake was seven. Jaz, Nina and Ayshea would be in their teens. With Jake at school, I would be able to take up a full-time position in a hospital.

I started to combine work, study and home life with the inevitable round of school visits, sports clubs, library visits, swimming and church. I did most of the studying in the evenings when the children were asleep. I found the medical course more interesting than anything I'd done at school, and as I realised I wasn't an academic failure, my confidence grew. I was exhausted, but happy.

I knew most of my neighbours by sight and to say hello to. One of them, a friend who used to childmind for me when I was at my course, asked me if I'd met X. She said he was staying with his uncle and aunt. I knew who they were – the uncle, who was Irish, worked in the building trade, which was thriving at that time. My neighbour said X had come over from Derry and had joined his uncle's squad. She said they were keen for him to meet people nearer his own age and were taking him out to the local pub and to friends' houses. She also said he was very handsome. I was introduced to him a few days later at another neighbour's house. I'd called in and X was there having a coffee. We got chatting. He was easy to talk to and very charming. I was instantly attracted to this handsome Irishman. He was clearly attracted to me, and I agreed to go out with him.

It was a rare treat to be taken out. That first date, I was smitten. He totally won me over. His aunt and uncle were delighted with the way things were turning out for us. They kept telling me that he was a hard worker and had been very good to them. Looking back, it seems that it all happened very quickly, but it felt so right. Within weeks, he'd moved in. I was on an emotional high. He was great with the children, who thought he was fantastic; he was supportive of me, helped round the house, and was very generous with his money. He almost never went out drinking – so much for the stereotypical Irish labourer, I thought. Three months later I was pregnant. It wasn't planned, but I'd let nature take its course. He was delighted and promised to support us all. As far as Trevor was concerned, if Jake was content, he was happy. Trevor never got involved in my private life.

There was another side to X – he could have quite a temper – but I loved him and pushed any worries to the back of my mind. After all, life was so good. I knew X had three children from two relationships back in Derry, and he missed them. But hadn't I four children myself? From two relationships that hadn't worked out? We had that in common. And any good father would obviously miss his children. He even went to Mass.

Christmas was coming. X told me he'd have to go back to Derry to see his family, especially the children. I wasn't worried. They all knew about me and had wished us well. I had my own family for Christmas. It's the best stage in any parent's life when Father Christmas still visits and everyone stays at home, playing party games, making decorations, baking cakes, watching Disney films together ... and my own parents were only a couple of miles away. Deborah and Stephen had settled further from home, so it was my children who enjoyed most of their grandparents' attention.

X had said he'd be back in January – the baby was due in February – but he didn't return. I'd tried to phone him over Christmas but hadn't been able to talk to him. I left messages but he didn't return my calls. I became more and more worried. Something had to be very wrong. He'd intended to see his children over the holiday and I suspected that there might have been some attempted reconciliation between X and his former partner. I knew he missed his children badly. My children were upset and I didn't know what to tell them. I rang his mother and sister. They told me that he had 'unfinished business' with the mother of his two younger children. They made it clear that they disapproved of her and were unhappy he had left me without any warning, especially when I was pregnant. They urged me to come over to Derry and work things out.

I was heartbroken but also determined not to give up easily. I kept in touch through X's family. The news wasn't good. It really upset me. They said he was drinking heavily, doing drugs, mixing with a bad crowd. He wouldn't get a job. They were describing a man the exact opposite of the one I'd known in England. They seemed to blame his children's mother – he was dividing his time between her house and a flat. I was tempted to agree. This was not the man I knew and loved. Whose baby I was carrying. The situation was incredibly stressful and in the middle of it all I was trying to study and look after the rest of my family. Something had to give. I gave up my studies. It was all too much.

X's family always answered my calls and told me something about what was going on in Derry, but I never heard from X again before J was born. Another very contented baby, fair and beautiful. I decided that when the summer came I would take up X's family's invitation and bring J to Derry.

When J and I went to Derry, Jaz, Nina and Ayshea stayed with Mum, while Jake stayed with his dad for the weekend, as usual. I didn't know what to expect but X's family greeted us with open arms and Irish hospitality. They assured me that I was the only one who could make X see sense. He agreed to meet me and was so pleased to see baby J that I felt hopeful. I had put off having J christened in the hope that the child's daddy could be there. The family introduced me to their priest, Father (now Monsignor) Brian McCanny, who was very pleasant to me. We arranged for a small christening to be held in a few weeks' time. X told me the relationship with his other children's mother was going nowhere and admitted he needed to sort things out. But he was adamant on one point – he was never going back to England. He was staying in Derry.

I came back for the christening in the late summer of 2001. X said his other relationship was over and we spent some time together. X's family urged me to put my name on the Housing Executive waiting list and said I'd have no problem getting a house. I went home to think it over.

If I was to make the move, I was determined on one thing – we were moving as a family. My only concern at this stage was Jake. I knew Trevor would not want him to move so far away, but I also knew I could talk to and negotiate with Trevor, unlike Sol. Sol had remarried – we divorced when I was twenty-five – and relations had all but broken down between us. Jaz and Nina didn't want to change schools or leave their friends, for the time being. So they would stay with my parents, as they had on my weekends away, and join me later – perhaps in the new term. And I would be back in England for a long weekend once a month, more if I could afford it, and stay with Mum and Dad. (If I was to apply for a house in Derry, I'd have to give up my council house in

Northampton.) Ayshea was determined to come with me as soon as her place at a Derry school was confirmed.

Then Trevor and I talked things through. Jake was four at the time. He was very close to his dad and Trevor lived for his son. We agreed that we would swap our arrangements. Jake would spend term-time with his dad and come to me in the school holidays. He would join us at my parents' house when I came over each month and he would also come to Derry for weekends with me.

So, as J, Ayshea and I arrived in Derry that October day, I was missing my elder children, Jaz and Nina, but anticipating them joining us later on. I wished that Jake was with me but I had always known that his time would be divided between Trevor and me. I felt happy that he had such a strong relationship with his dad, and it was important that his first year at school was as settled as possible. I had no concerns for his welfare and knew that, with phone calls, the time would fly until we all met up again. Mum and Dad would miss us, but were enjoying the company of the older ones who were past the stage of hands-on care. Finally, it seemed, I was being given the opportunity to make a fresh start and to build a better life for us all, in a beautiful part of the country. How could I have been so wrong? But then, how could I have foreseen what lay ahead?

It All Goes Wrong

We started out staying with X's sister-in-law in the Carnhill area of Derry, and I put my name down on the housing list. Ayshea enrolled in Carnhill High School. J and I joined a Mums and Tots group and also Sure Start, a government programme that provides various parents' courses and supports early learning activities for pre-school children. Within a month I had the tenancy of a lovely house in Fernabbey, and set about making it a real home.

X was living in a flat but spending more and more time with us. I continued to worry about the changes I saw in him. I still loved him, but there were aspects of his behaviour in Derry that I could not like. He had no inclination to get a job and provide for his family. And he went out socialising a lot. From Thursday to Sunday, it was one long party; he was drinking far too much. I suspected he was also taking drugs. His family insisted I was the right person to help him sort himself out and did everything they could to support me.

I went back with J and Ayshea to England in February 2002, to my parents' house. I already knew I was pregnant again and was looking forward to sharing the news. But our reception was not what I had expected. Mum hadn't been keeping too well. She was suffering from stress and tiredness, and bouts of depression. I don't think she had ever fully grieved for her own mother, my nan, who had died in 2000, and it was starting to take its toll on her health. Crucially, she hadn't told me that Jaz and Nina, albeit well-behaved, were simply getting to be too much for her. Just before I got back, she'd contacted Sol and sent them to him.

Sol and his new wife wouldn't have been expecting this. Maybe it upset their own plans. Sol and I hadn't talked in years so he knew very little about X, and about life in Derry. I hadn't felt any need to tell him about my plans to move the family to Ireland. After all, we were divorced. But when Mum had asked Sol to have Jaz and Nina live with him, he was immediately involved again. He didn't want his children moving so far away from him, from my parents, from the lifestyle and friends they knew. He didn't know much about Ireland and what he did know wasn't positive. He had heard about X and he didn't want the older children coming under the influence of a man he didn't know. So he was determined to stop them leaving England. He filed for custody. He was a wealthy man and he was able to afford the best lawyers. Suddenly he started lavishing the children with expensive gifts and giving them generous sums of cash in a bid to persuade them to stay in England. Mum was always fond of Sol, in spite of everything, and they had stayed in touch. This crisis brought them closer. She shared his impression of Ireland and, like him, was afraid of losing Nina, Jaz and Ayshea for good. While I'd known that she had been run down, Mum's decision that she couldn't cope with Jaz and Nina had come out of the blue and she was grateful that Sol had been there to take them in. I still have no idea why she didn't talk to me before she did this.

When I arrived in Northampton, I was met by a summons to attend a Family Court for an emergency custody hearing. I got a solicitor and discovered that Jaz, Nina and Ayshea were forbidden by law from leaving the country until the case was decided. Derry is part of the UK but Northern Ireland has its own legislation in many cases.

I challenged Mum about what had happened. She admitted she had never wanted the children and me to move to Ireland. She said she had helped me to bring them up, and she would miss them so much. She thought of Ireland as a rather strange, faraway place and couldn't understand why I liked it. Unlike Mum, Dad was born a Catholic, but neither really understood my faith and why I'd enrolled Ayshea at a Catholic school. They weren't happy about my relationship with X, and were worried about whether it would work out. If it didn't, I think they saw no point in me staying in Ireland and felt it was wrong to move Jaz, Nina and Ayshea in the meantime.

While I can understand why Mum chose to support Sol's point of view, it hurt me a lot. I felt betrayed and let down. She knew how little he'd done for the children over the past few years. She knew he hadn't paid maintenance, and that he was only showering them all with gifts and money now to get them on his side in the court case. I felt she'd been bought over, too, and my feelings of betrayal took a long time to heal.

When it was time to go back to Derry, I had to leave Ayshea in Northampton, because the court order did not allow her to leave the country. I travelled back and forth to England every month, which was as often as I could afford. Mum continued to make it clear that she was definitely backing Sol on this one. She wanted me to move back to Northampton. I applied for emergency housing there to have a base from which to fight my court case, as she said she wasn't well enough to have J and me staying with her. All I got was a place in a refuge. This was understandable, as I had a local authority house in Ireland.

When we got to court, about eight weeks later, Sol agreed that I was a very good mother. He admitted he'd been an absent father a lot of the time and hadn't paid maintenance. He saw no reason to oppose me having custody, but had taken this case to stop me moving the children to Ireland. He spoke of the disruption to their education, about taking them away from their grandparents, their friends, and from him. The judge saw no reason to stop me having custody, either, so I won the case. But it was on the grounds that I moved back to England so that the children's education and their family ties weren't disrupted. It didn't seem to matter that Ayshea's education had already been disrupted when she'd had to leave her school in Derry. There was no custody case over J, so J's family ties weren't considered.

I went back to Derry with a heavy heart. Jake came over for part of the summer and enjoyed his time in Derry; he's the kind of child who makes new friends easily and he was happy to spend time with J and me. We travelled back and forth often to Northampton to see Jaz, Nina and Ayshea. X was now living with us most of the time but the relationship wasn't good. I found I couldn't trust him. Alongside my worries about his drinking, I suspected that he was seeing other women.

I'd made friends with an extended family who lived nearby. I was especially friendly with Janice, who lived with her four children, her partner and her two adult brothers. Her children got on well with J and with my other children when they came to visit. She'd had her share of problems, too, and became a good friend. I needed her very much in the last weeks of my pregnancy.

X and I were rowing all the time. I couldn't cope with his disruptive, aggressive and drunken behaviour, not when I was caring for J and about to give birth. In the end, he walked out days before I went into labour. I was relieved. The house was peaceful again. I knew the relationship was over and had been for some time. Janice looked after J and came to Altnagelvin Hospital with me, where, in September 2002, I gave birth to another fair-haired baby, K. A perfectly healthy, contented baby.

Altnagelvin Hospital

The nightmare began in the early afternoon of Saturday, 19 October 2002.

It should have been a happy day, spent, like every other, at my home in Fernabbey, with my two youngest children. It's a housing development a few miles from the city centre that was originally built for the private market, but was now run by a housing scheme. There were plenty of young families living there and quite a few single parents. I was on nodding terms with most of my neighbours but Janice was my only close friend. I'd been there for almost a year, but I'd been travelling frequently, back and forth, between Derry and Northampton during that time. I'm quite a shy person deep down.

I was happy at home. X had gone, putting an end to the rows, and the house was so much more peaceful now. The days had settled into a round of feeding, changing, washing and cleaning, and making sure there was time when K was asleep to concentrate on J, who was almost two. J was a contented child who enjoyed me reading a story, having a cuddle, playing with toys, and was very affectionate towards the new arrival. I'd often call over to Janice's or she'd visit me for a coffee but, apart from that, I rarely went further than the local shops or the church. Father McCanny visited the house when he was doing his parish rounds. I enjoyed his company. I sometimes found the community I lived in a little insular and he'd chat away about things he'd read in the English papers.

The older children had been on the phone, wanting all the news about the baby, and looking forward to the time when the three of us could fly to Northampton for a few days. Mum's health had improved and relations between us were settling down again. I knew that I'd have to consider seriously moving back to Northampton, at some stage. I couldn't afford to keep flying over and back again. I was very reluctant to leave Derry and still hoped that perhaps I could persuade Jaz, Nina and Ayshea to join me for the summer holidays. This wasn't unrealistic. Sol had told the court that I was a good mother; if I had moved back to England, all three of our children would have been back with me full-time. Sol never denied me access, and he had never tried to get sole custody of the children. I could see no reason why he would object to them spending the summer holidays with me, in Ireland. And if Sol didn't object, the courts wouldn't either. Jake was happy to come in the holidays and was looking forward to meeting K.

I was never sorry that I'd moved to Derry, but I did regret I had not foreseen that Sol would go to court to try to stop the children joining me. That was totally unexpected, and I still believe it was motivated by spite. But for the next few months, I had to put any final decisions on hold as I cared for a lively toddler and a new baby, single-handed.

X's family were nearby but once they realised our relationship was over for good, and that he didn't seem interested in having access to his children, they disappeared out of our life – for the time being. Janice was a lifeline. Her home was always busy, with her sisters and friends calling round. She'd been urging me to get dressed up a bit and have a night out away from the babies, saying it would do me good to have a break. She knew she was the only person I would trust to babysit.

Her brother Peter was due to play in a darts match in a local pub one Friday night and most of her family were going along to support him. Janice persuaded me to join them. Although I don't usually enjoy pubs or clubs, I agreed. That evening, I took J and K over to Janice's house, where her family were gathering for a drink. I had a few sips of beer while I got the children settled for the night, then went off with the group. During the evening, I sipped at a couple of Malibu and Cokes, but didn't finish them. I enjoyed the company but wasn't really in form for a late night. Then Peter and his mother got involved in a heated argument. After that, I just wanted to get back to the children as soon as I could.

Both J and K were sound asleep when we got back to Janice's. She was in bed, too, so I sat and chatted to her other brother for a while. He helped me carry the children the hundred yards to my house. I settled J on the sofa without waking the child and put the cot down beside it. I was absolutely shattered. I slipped off my shoes and cuddled up beside J, pulling a duvet over us both, and fell asleep. I managed to get about three hours sleep before it was time for K's next bottle.

The next day, at around 11.30 a.m., I went in a taxi to the Post Office to cash my Giro cheque. I took both of the children, leaving baby K in the taxi while I ran into the Post Office with J. Just after I got home, at around noon, Peter called round to apologise for the row the night before. He knew it had upset me and he was embarrassed. I told him not to worry about it. I offered him a coffee but then realised there was no milk in the house. I popped out to the local shop, just a few minutes away, leaving the children with Peter. When I got back, Peter and I had a coffee together and then he went home.

Baby K had been a bit unsettled that day, and looked rather pale, but I wondered if it just seemed like that because I was tired myself. After Peter had gone, K wouldn't settle for me, not at all. No amount of winding or carrying about seemed to help. I wondered if it could be colic. Then the baby gave a cry that didn't sound like anything I'd heard before. Instinctively I knew something wasn't right. I wrapped up the baby and J and we walked over to Janice's house to see what she thought. She had several visitors and all of them agreed with me that the baby was very pale and didn't look well. I decided to ring the doctor, so I went back home and called the emergency number at my health centre. The doctor on duty advised me to bring the baby straight over, so I gathered up a few things – a bottle and nappy – went back to Janice's and she drove us over.

On the way, I held K tight but the baby was becoming very cold and lifeless. I started to panic. I hurried into the surgery, where I was met by the duty doctor, Dr A. He examined the baby immediately. Lying on the couch, K was such a tiny little thing, limp and deathly pale. I was terrified that my baby, who had been such a lively little soul the day before, was slipping away before my eyes and there was nothing I could do to help. I looked hopelessly at Dr A. He said he wanted the baby admitted to Altnagelvin Hospital at once. I told him my friend had a car waiting outside, so he sent us ahead while he rang to tell the hospital we were on our way. He couldn't tell me what was wrong – only that K was very ill. He later said that he'd decided on an emergency admission within seconds of seeing K.

Janice drove as fast as was sensible to the A & E entrance of the hospital. It was a ten-minute journey and the roads were fairly quiet but, to me, it seemed to take forever. The medical team was waiting for me as I rushed in, carrying K in my arms. A doctor took K's temperature. A nurse looked me in the eye and warned me, quietly, that I had a 'very sick baby'. I asked what the reading was and the doctor told me the baby's temperature didn't register. A terrible chill ran through me. Did that mean K was dying? The staff told me it was a good thing we'd been sent straight to them. There is no doubt that Dr A's prompt action saved K's life.

A consultant radiologist, Dr D, examined K. I didn't catch his name at the time and I wouldn't have remembered his face but, unknown to me then, he would turn out to be our guardian angel. He didn't say anything to me directly, but he told his colleague, Dr B, the consultant paediatrician at Altnagelvin, that he thought K had a form of childhood cancer called a neuroblastoma.

I didn't see K again until about seven o'clock that evening – I will never forget it, K was wrapped up in a silver blanket and with a baby hat on. A nurse explained that it was to keep K warm while they carried out tests. The next time I saw K, around nine o'clock, the baby was in an incubator. K's tummy was very swollen and K was very distressed. I remember putting my finger in baby K's hand and K clasped it very tight. The medical staff explained to me that they would put K on a drip, try to raise the baby's temperature and monitor the condition every few minutes. I stayed beside the incubator, watching and praying.

Janice had taken J home with her, trying to explain as calmly as she could that the baby was sick and Mummy had to stay at the hospital. She came back later and told me that J was fine. X's mother arrived and stayed for a while.

It was touch and go that night. I stayed by K, only

catching a few minutes' sleep in the chair by the incubator. I was so frightened, watching out for any tiny changes in the baby's colour, any signs of movement, any little cry. K had been a healthy seven-pound baby at birth but now looked so frail and helpless, so vulnerable. The nursing staff were wonderful, kind and supportive, bringing me cups of tea and answering my questions, even encouraging me to go to the parents' room for a couple of hours' sleep. But I wouldn't leave K's side. It had all happened so suddenly. I was still in a state of shock.

Other anxious relatives were coming and going through the twilight world of the hospital's emergency unit. I will always remember the kindness one woman showed me, a total stranger. Seeing my desperation, as I mouthed silent prayers at the bedside, she took a little card from her bag and gave it to me. It was a prayer to Saint Teresa. It is one of my most treasured possessions.

Somehow K made it through the night. The next morning, the Sunday, there were more tests, including a scan. At around ten o'clock Dr B told me, gently, that they'd detected bleeding in the kidney area; K had a tumour above the kidney. This was typical of a neuroblastoma, or cancer. I'd never heard of a neuroblastoma. My first thought was of leukaemia. But the impact was the same. I tried to hold back the sobs but my heart was racing in terror. Cancer. The word everyone dreads. Did this mean my baby was dying? He told me that K needed an operation and as there was no paediatric surgeon available at Altnagelvin, they were discussing K's transfer to the Royal Belfast Hospital for Sick Children and planning it for the next day.

Janice came back to the hospital, and then X arrived and some of his extended family. In the afternoon I went home to get clothes for me and K. I called to Janice's house to see J, who was fine. While I was there, X rang me and asked if the hospital could give K a blood transfusion. I told him they could and hurried back to Altnagelvin. K was deteriorating and the hospital made the decision to do the transfer that day. I could travel the seventy-odd miles in the ambulance with my baby, who was still attached to a drip.

As they prepared K for the journey I never felt more alone. X had left; his mum and sister decided not to make the journey with me. Janice had gone home to look after J and I rang her to tell her what was happening.

We set off in the ambulance not knowing what lay ahead. I sat with K, Saint Teresa's prayer card held tightly in my hand, and, as we sped along the road to Belfast, I fervently prayed for my baby's recovery.

The Royal Belfast Hospital for Sick Children

We arrived at the Royal at about 11 p.m. and were greeted by Dr C. He explained that K had been transferred there in case the baby needed surgery because of the neuroblastoma. K was taken for a blood transfusion. The medical staff said the baby had been bleeding internally. They wanted to carry out more tests and told me that I should have a definite diagnosis by the Tuesday.

A nurse suggested that I should get some sleep and set up a bed in an unused ward. This was to be my home for the next two weeks. She assured me she would wake me up immediately if there was any change in K. I was exhausted, frantic with worry, and lay down thinking I would never get to sleep. The next thing I knew it was 6.30 a.m. I went straight to K, still looking so small and helpless in the incubator.

Later that morning X arrived from Derry and said he planned to stay while K was ill. I didn't contact anyone apart from Janice. I didn't want to leave K's side. Besides, what could I tell my family? All I knew was that the baby might have cancer.

That day was hectic with doctors and nurses doing tests on K. I kept my vigil at K's bedside, clutching my prayer card like a talisman, willing my tiny baby to cling to life. Gradually, I thought I saw a little colour returning. It was hard to tell. It could have been wishful thinking. I felt helpless, and alone. Utterly exhausted, I went to bed that night to try to get some sleep. X and I were to get the test results the next day and would hear what the doctors had found out about K's illness.

The next morning K was beginning to improve a little. The doctors were as good as their word and gave us some test results. They said the baby's left kidney and the area around it were swollen. There had been internal bleeding in the area, which had formed a mass that showed up on the scan. But they couldn't agree on what had caused the bleeding in the first place. I was exhausted and stressed, and had eaten practically nothing. I struggled to take it in. One doctor came to me and told me that K had a tumour. Another doctor diagnosed cancer, and mentioned the word 'leukaemia'.

That Tuesday morning, Dr C called X and me into a side room. I didn't know why. I wondered if it was to break bad news to us in private. Instead, he confronted me. He asked me if I had done anything to hurt my baby. He said he had called in the social services and the police because K had a non-accidental injury that had to be reported. They would be here, shortly, to speak to me.

I couldn't believe what I was hearing. Even in my exhausted state I was indignant. How could they suspect me? The nursing staff had seen K's records and commented on how well the baby had been cared for. I comforted myself by saying it must be a terrible mistake. Surely, the next time they examined the baby, it'd all become clear and this misunderstanding would be sorted out. All that mattered was that K would get better.

Later, I would hear it confirmed in court that, in fact, only one doctor who examined K was definite in his opinion that the baby had been deliberately assaulted. Others who came round to his diagnosis could not agree on when such an injury had been sustained. It could have been anything from twenty-four hours to just one hour before K was admitted to Altnagelvin. Most thought it was probably around six hours before K's admission – say, early morning to around noon.

X left the room to phone his mum. When he came back, he said he was leaving. His mum had advised him to go. 'You don't think I hurt K?' I asked him. 'Someone has,' he said. I rang my sister Deborah and told her what was happening. She tried to reassure me, saying I had nothing to worry about, that everyone would know I'd never hurt K.

Nothing made any sense. First it was cancer; then,

someone had hurt K. I felt numb. A social worker based in the hospital called to talk to me. She was very nice and said that she didn't think I'd hurt K. There was also a woman doctor who said that in her opinion K was well cared for.

All the time I had been at K's bedside, I thought things were fine in Derry. I had to keep my mobile phone switched off to avoid interference with the medical equipment. But when I'd taken a break outside, I'd rung Janice and she told me that some of X's family had come round to her house and had insisted on taking J to stay with them. Janice wasn't happy about this, as she didn't think I'd want J to go there, but X was the child's father, so she had agreed. She didn't leave me a phone message about this because she thought I had enough to worry about.

I was angry with her at first for letting X's family take J. But she said they'd put her under pressure and there was nothing she could do. Tearfully, I told her about what I was being accused of. She couldn't believe it. Like me, she thought it must be a terrible mistake. She encouraged me to be positive – all that mattered was that K, who had been so close to death, was now getting better.

Meanwhile, the social services team in Derry were putting in place the standard 'preventative' measures they use when a parent is suspected of harming their child. They went to X's family's home on that Tuesday and gave them the choice of having the care and custody of J while the investigation was carried out, or handing over the toddler to the Foyle Trust for short-term foster care. J was placed in foster care and was collected by social workers a short time later. As far as I knew, J was still safe and well at Janice's house. No one told me what was going on.

The police and the duty social worker arrived at the hospital that Tuesday evening. First, two police officers asked me questions about what had happened before K fell ill. I went over things as best I could but it was clear they were convinced that someone had assaulted the baby. And that someone was most likely me, or someone I was covering up for. Then it was the turn of the social worker. He explained that until the police investigation was completed I wouldn't be allowed to care for my older child. This was just a precautionary procedure, he assured me. So J was now in short-term foster care in Derry and the social services would arrange a visit for me when I was back home. There was nothing I could do about it.

I was devastated. What must little J be thinking? The toddler was too young to understand where Mummy was, and why. Couldn't they see I was a good mother? What kind of person would do this to a month-old baby? Why would I harm my own child, and why would I tell lies to cover up for someone else? I felt sick at the thought that they must see me as some sort of monster. The nursing staff did their best to be kind. They kept telling me that K was a lovely baby, and had been well cared for.

Things weren't helped when X turned up at the hospital again on Wednesday, and with some of his family. He can be outspoken and aggressive. I think he had been drinking. He didn't ask to see me or the baby. He was being abusive about the fact that someone had assaulted his baby and he wanted to know who it was. The medical staff asked him to leave.

After a six-day, round-the-clock vigil, K's condition had improved a lot. What a joy it was to be able to cuddle my baby again, and to give my infant its bottle. At no stage did anyone try to stop me caring for my child. Seeing K restored to life, animated and content, made all the sleepless nights and stressful days worthwhile. I was told that we'd soon be transferred back to Altnagelvin.

Three weeks later, my life had settled into a new routine. Most of my time was spent at Altnagelvin Hospital, either at K's bedside, feeding, cuddling and changing, or dozing in the parents' room. I remember there was a musical mobile above K's cot, which K loved. I'd wind it up over and over again and K would look up in delight as the soft toys bobbed slowly round and round. It was the firm favourite from the hospital toys.

But I was very upset about J. I hadn't been able to see my child at all. I wanted to try to explain what had happened, to give a hug, anything. Social services gave me a message that J was well. I couldn't contact the foster family – that was not encouraged or acceptable. I was told I would be given an access visit, in a community building, later.

When I went back to Fernabbey to do my washing, pick up fresh clothes and check the post. I'd usually call in with Janice to tell her what was happening and she also visited the hospital. I called at my house one day, I remember the date – 14 November 2002.

When they saw me arrive, my neighbours told me the police had been there, looking for me, the day before.

I knew the police were waiting to interview me formally. I also knew that if they thought I had harmed K and intended to take me to court, K would not be allowed to come home with me when discharged from hospital. K would be taken into foster care like J had been. I couldn't even let myself start to think about this. I had no idea how to convince them I was innocent. I had no idea who could have harmed my baby. The very idea of it made me so angry. And what about the doctors who had told me K had cancer? I'd been so worried that K was going to die. Did this mean K hadn't had cancer after all?

Another consequence, and also a part of their standard procedures, was that social services in Derry got in touch with the authorities in Northampton to let them know the situation with J and K. As I was suspected of harming K, I was informed that I would now only be allowed to see Jaz, Nina, Ayshea and Jake under supervision and only at my parents' house. I wasn't allowed to be on my own with my children, I wasn't allowed to take them out anywhere and they certainly weren't able to visit me in Derry.

I didn't know what to tell my family in Northampton because I didn't know myself.

Even in my state of complete mental and physical exhaustion, I grasped one fact. I would have to get myself a solicitor.

Finding Carmel

It must have been fate that brought Carmel McGilloway
and me together. I knew I had to get a solicitor but I had
no idea how to go about choosing one. Somewhere at the
back of my mind I recalled a conversation I'd heard,
perhaps in Janice's house, where someone had said
Brendan Kearney's firm of solicitors had done a good job.
So I thought I'd try them. Their offices are in Clarendon
Street in Derry, near the city centre. I tried to convince
myself that they must be able to sort something out and
clear up this terrible misunderstanding. But inside I was
feeling wretched. I was overtired, worn out, and lonely.
I thought nobody else could understand how much this
hurt. My two-year-old taken from me without even a
chance to say goodbye or to give a cuddle. There seemed
no doubt now that the same thing was going to happen
to the baby. I knew I should be grateful that K had made
such a good recovery when only three weeks ago the baby
had been at death's door. I'd almost lost the little one.

Was I now going to lose my baby to something else? It was hard to fight the misery I felt and the self-pity.

Brendan Kearney's receptionist referred me to their family law practitioner, Carmel McGilloway. I was lucky – she could see me straightaway. I was shown in to her office. The woman who shook my hand was seven months' pregnant – not what I expected but I remember thinking, 'Well, at least she's a mother too – she might understand.' Carmel told me this would be her third child. That set the pattern for our relationship – she is a brilliant solicitor but she never loses sight of the fact that she is also a woman and a mother and that some humanity counts for a lot.

Carmel says now that her first impression of me was of someone who was very vulnerable. She says that when I walked into her consulting room, I cut a pitiful figure. As soon as I spoke she realised from my accent that I was far from home. She encouraged me to tell my story; I know I wasn't anything like as clear or concise as I should have been. Everything that had been building up inside me came out in a jumbled rush – facts, thoughts, worries, fears. But Carmel listened, pausing now and then to take a few notes or check on something I'd said. She told me I was 'stoic'. I thought I was anything but, though her words gave me strength and confidence. Maybe we could fight this. I was never one to lie down in a crisis.

Carmel says that while it's not a solicitor's job to decide whether a client is innocent or guilty, she believed, from that first meeting, that I was telling her the truth and she really wanted to help me. Later on, in court, when things seemed to be going against us, she told me that one big thing in my favour was that my story had never changed. No matter how often I had to go over the details, it never changed. My emotional state was to be more of a problem. Carmel admits now that during police interviews and later in the courtroom I came across as very calm – she used the word 'detached'. She says I seemed cut off from my emotions. There was no shouting, no screaming and crying, none of the extremes of emotion she might have expected from a mother who had given birth just two months earlier and had had two of her children taken from her. To some people it might seem that I just didn't care that much, that I was a cold person who had no strong feelings for my children. No great maternal instinct.

Nothing could have been further than the truth, but I know what she means. It's been my way of coping with loss and pain. When there's a situation I can't do anything about, I block myself off from it. I try to keep my emotions at bay. It's a deliberate thing. I know that if I'd allowed myself to dwell on what had happened with J and K or to think that I might never get my babies back, or that I might even be sent to prison, I wouldn't have been able to cope. I'd have broken down completely. I wouldn't have been able to fight my corner. And I had to keep fighting – for myself, for my children, and for the truth.

I asked Carmel what would happen to me. She advised

me to let her ring the police station and make an appointment for us to go there together the next day. She said they'd caution me and then ask me questions about what had happened before K was admitted to hospital – who'd been alone with the baby, things like that. She reassured me that it was the usual practice for any siblings to be taken into care in case they were at risk. I was starting to realise that the Foyle Health and Social Services Trust had a great deal of power.

I left Carmel's office and spent the rest of the day and the night at the hospital and forced myself to concentrate on enjoying being with little K rather than worrying about whether I was going to have the baby taken away. Still, my mood would swing from despair, to anxiety about the future, to frustration that the social services and the police couldn't see what was so obvious to the nursing staff – that I was a good and loving mother.

Carmel might have described me as 'stoic' and 'strong' but I was shaking all over when we walked towards Strand Road police station the next day. She had made me a coffee in her office, given me a few last words of re-assurance, and now, here we were, just around the corner and about to walk through the metal gates. My stomach was churning, my hands were trembling. I was sure I was talking gibberish. The security gates closed behind us. I was terrified.

We reported in at the front desk at around eleven o'clock. Minutes later, two female police officers from the Care Unit at Maydown arrived and took us into a small room for questioning. This unit, in the Waterside area of Derry, deals with cases involving vulnerable adults and children, and sexual crimes. Its officers are said to be trained to handle their inquiries empathically and sensitively. A large proportion of them are women. Carmel had warned me that I would be formally cautioned, and that this was usual procedure. But nothing could have prepared me for the endless barrage of questions. The police officers wanted me to go through the events of the twenty-four hours before K was admitted to hospital. Over and over again, the same repetitive questions. I gave them the same answers. I found them cold and very official. I felt from the start that they thought I was guilty. It seemed to go on for a long, long time before they took a break for lunch.

Then the real panic set in. Carmel told me that the policy when an interview is interrupted in order for the police to have a meal break is to place the suspect temporarily in a cell. I'm a bit claustrophobic and I was really alarmed at the prospect of being locked in a small cell. Carmel had a word with the officers and they agreed to move me to a bigger cell and to leave the door open. They also gave me a magazine to read, to pass the hour's wait. Not that I could concentrate, but it was a gesture. Carmel reminded me that she had an appointment that afternoon but that her colleague, Philomena Melaugh, would be with me before the interview resumed.

In the afternoon, in Philomena's presence, I was questioned for about four hours by two male officers from the

CID. The same questions. Time and time again I went over what had happened in the hours before we went to Altnagelvin. I'd gone over those same details myself, many, many times. I was searching for my own clues about what could have happened to K. Didn't the police realise that I was as determined as they were to find out what had happened to my baby, who had so nearly died?

The detectives told me that the doctor who had raised the alarm at the Royal, Dr C, believed that K had suffered a non-accidental injury. And that K had been assaulted within six hours of being admitted to Altnagelvin. It could be as long as twenty-four hours, but it was more probably six, or even less. Who else had been alone with K? Again, I got the impression they thought it could only have been me.

I was questioned for a total of around six hours that day. It left me drained. When they'd finished, the detectives told me they would release me on my own bail of five hundred pounds while they continued with their inquiries. I panicked about this until Philomena assured me I wouldn't have to produce the sum in cash before I could go. The detectives warned me I should expect to be called back in for interview at a later date.

Carmel had already explained to me that everything I'd been questioned about so far related to a criminal case, which the police were building. It was all about bringing to trial in Londonderry Crown Court the person who had assaulted K. I would also be facing a second court case, in the Family Division of the High Court in Belfast.

This would involve social workers investigating my record as a parent, and my lifestyle, and then putting forward a case as to whether the children should be returned to me or remain in foster care. I had to face the fact that, while I was a suspect, K was also going to be fostered. And, for now, I could do nothing to stop it.

Later that month, the dreadful day arrived. I'd been involved with a number of different social workers and they'd told me I would have a day's notice to allow me to get ready a bag of some of K's favourite things to take to the foster parents. The night before, I'd wept uncontrollably as I'd packed K's little clothes, a favourite Mickey Mouse cuddly toy, and a note to the couple who would become Mummy and Daddy for the foreseeable future. I wrote down everything I could think of – that the baby had colicky attacks at six in the evening and should be rocked to sleep. That the baby needed to be coaxed to take milk. That the baby was very much loved. I dressed K in my favourite outfit and hugged my baby close. At least J and K would be together in the same foster home. It was small consolation, but I clung to it. I willed myself not to think.

Then, at two o'clock in the afternoon, in that most anonymous and sterile of settings, the time came to kiss my baby goodbye. Social workers quickly took K out of the hospital ward and down the corridor. I watched them disappear in the direction of the lift. I couldn't move. My legs wouldn't function. But K's cot was being changed, another baby would be admitted, and it was time for me to go. I was left to make my way across town, through the bitter cold of the autumn evening, home to an empty, silent house. There was no welcome there. An empty cot, and an empty bed, devoid of the love and life and laughter of my two-year-old. A home my baby would never remember. It was the loneliest journey of my life. I truly thought my heart would break.

Counting My Friends

Out on bail, I retreated to my home in Ferndale Drive and locked the door. I more or less kept it locked for the next eight months. I shut out the world. Derry was gearing itself up for Christmas and I wanted no part of it. All around the estate, Christmas trees twinkled in lighted windows, and 'Santa Stop Here' signs were stuck in the smallest gardens and beside front doors. Christmas carols were playing everywhere. The crib went up in the church, the Advent candles were lit one by one. I steeled myself to ignore it. Even if I had managed to put on a brave face, who was I putting it on for?

An official letter informed me that my social security benefit was being cut. Obviously, since J and K no longer lived with me, their child allowance would be paid to the foster family. I still had my tenancy and a single person's allowance. I was living on around fifty pounds a week. Carmel had applied for legal aid to cover my costs.

She'd also reminded me that she'd be on maternity

leave by the time the police contacted me again, as it would probably take several months for them to complete their investigations. They'd want to interview everyone who'd been with baby K in the twenty-four hours before the hospital admission. They'd also want to talk to my health visitor and perhaps other health professionals.

I was trying to come to terms with the fact that I could well be facing two separate court cases: one, if the police charged me with a criminal offence; the other, a Family Court to decide the best way to care for my children. I couldn't believe this was happening. All because I'd done what any responsible, caring parent would do – taken a very sick baby to the doctor. For now there was nothing I could do except wait.

To say I was at an all-time low doesn't even begin to describe the state I was in. I'd been used to a busy routine caring for J and was just starting to adapt it to the needs of the new baby. With two youngsters under three, there's never a spare moment – or a dull one. Or a quiet one. Now the house was too big, too empty, too silent. Long days stretched ahead of me with no purpose in them. I ached for J and K, growing up such a short distance away from me but in a different world. I lay on the sofa and cried, I missed them so much. I couldn't let myself dwell on the trial, or what would happen if I was convicted and went to prison. My imagination would run riot. I could feel the panic rising inside me and I'd tell myself, stop, *stop* … Sometimes it all seemed unreal, like it was happening to someone else. I don't think I made a decision to cut myself off. It was a survival mechanism kicking in.

These were the coldest and the darkest months of the year. I couldn't afford to heat the house and there wasn't much money to buy food. What little I had I spent on my visits with the children, three times a week, for a ninety-minute supervised meeting. I tried to walk the mile and a half from Fernabbey to Shantallow, but if the weather was very bad, I'd spend a couple of pounds on the bus. A taxi cost five pounds for the return trip – fifteen pounds a week was an impossible sum of money. I was allowed to buy them little gifts. I tried to budget for phone credit, too, to keep in touch with Northampton.

At home, I retreated into the living room. I never went into the upstairs bedrooms. The sight of their cuddly toys, their empty bed and cot, little clothes folded away in the drawers, was just too unbearably sad. I slept on the sofa, day and night, wrapped up in J's favourite Winnie-the-Pooh duvet for comfort and for warmth. After a few washes, it no longer carried J's distinctive baby smell. I missed that, too. I had no appetite. I couldn't be bothered to cook or to go to the shops for fresh, healthy food. The mother who had insisted that her children would learn good eating habits now got by on mugs of coffee and the odd biscuit or two. I've never been heavy but now the weight dropped off me. Sometimes I'd switch on the television for company, but I couldn't concentrate on it. I couldn't concentrate on anything. All the traditional Christmas and New Year specials full of happy parents and laughing children reminded me of what I'd lost. And I hadn't done anything wrong, I had to remind myself. I was living every mother's nightmare. And I couldn't wake up.

Very soon, there was another reason not to go outside my front door. I'd given the police all the information I could about what had happened on the day and night before K became so very ill. Now the detectives would be interviewing my friends – Janice, Peter and her family. Suspicions arose that I'd blamed them for harming K. Several of X's relatives lived near me and they lost no time in telling people their version of what had happened. That X's baby had been 'battered' and that both X's children had been taken off me and put into care. That the police had been at my door. They'd made their minds up. I was guilty. When I did venture out to the shop or to get the bus or a taxi to Shantallow for a visit with the children, I was conscious of heads turning away from me. People who I knew to see wouldn't meet my gaze. They looked down at the pavement, or crossed the road out of my way. It couldn't all have been paranoia. I was that Englishwoman who had committed the most hateful crime. I had nearly killed my own baby. I was made to feel like an outcast. Nobody spoke, nobody asked how I was. I sensed people hoped I'd just disappear.

The social services arranged the visits with the children. The format never varied. The visits were held in a room in Shantallow Health Centre and supervised by a social worker. I was never allowed to be alone with my children.

The room was basic and functional, designed for public meetings. There was a handful of old and well-worn toys. I wasn't allowed to bring any of their things from home. Someone else had bathed the children, chosen their clothes and dressed them, made them their meal before they were brought to meet me. It was impossible to create any sort of family atmosphere in that room. But I had to accept it. It was all I had.

J was always delighted to see me and the smile on that little face and the outstretched arms gave me precious memories to keep me going until the next visit. It was hard to find ways to keep J entertained – the toys weren't appealing – so I made up games using the sink, some plastic tumblers, a little water and a lot of imagination. Holding J close, we'd cuddle and play together. J was old enough to know that something was wrong when Mummy Louise, as I'd been told to call myself, was only there now and again and in this strange place. But not old enough to understand why.

Toddlers have a low boredom threshold and the room was uncomfortable; the ever-present eye of social services made the visits unnatural. Still, I never missed a visit. I was determined to make the best of them. With little K, it was a pleasure to see the baby thriving after being so ill. K was on no medical treatment at all and had never shown any signs of ill health since being discharged from hospital. The illness itself remained a mystery. Cuddles and hugs were wonderful. I couldn't fault the way my children were being cared for. Except that it wasn't me doing the caring. The social worker told me that the foster mother had said that, after each visit, J would sit at the window and cry for me, for hours. Nothing could comfort the child. That broke my heart. Again.

I tried to get across to my family in England what was happening. But they were far away and couldn't do anything about it. I couldn't afford to fly over to join them for Christmas. Again, I felt let down. I wished that somehow they'd have raised the money to buy me a ticket. Mum and Dad were enjoying the company of four of their grandchildren and it would have made a big difference to me to have been with them all. I had to settle for a brief phone call. I had no chance to explain in detail what was going on. Sometimes I wondered if any of them cared. Was this my 'punishment' for going to Ireland? Dad had made a point of saying he believed me. Mum said that if I was telling the truth, everything would be all right. I'd never been close to my brother Stephen who had moved to Devon before I'd even left home. We hadn't kept in touch. I was a bit closer to my sister Deborah.

Christmas was bleak. I wasn't allowed to see the children over the holiday. The day before Christmas Eve I was back in court to get an injunction against X. He'd turned up at my door, drunk, aggressive and shouting abuse. It was the first time he'd done it but it was enough to get a barring order imposed on him. Christmas Day itself passed in a blur. I lay on the sofa, trying to block out the world.

My only visitor at this time was Father McCanny. He

still included me in his round of parish visits, bringing me news of the world beyond Fernabbey. It was the only mental stimulus I had. He always had time to listen to me and never judged me. I hadn't been going to Mass in the local church because I didn't want to bump into X's family or face the scandal-mongers. But early in the new year, after each contact visit with the children, I started walking from Shantallow to Carnhill chapel, where no one knew me. I'd sit there for hours, breathing in the peace and tranquillity. It was the perfect place to sit and think, to try to put my life in perspective. I felt so safe there. It truly was a refuge and safe haven from the pain of the world. My prayer was simple and never altered: 'Please God let the truth be told. Nothing else.' If regular worshippers wondered about me, this woman who sat for hours on end, they never passed comment. Some of them exchanged a smile, or a nod of casual recognition. It meant a lot to me.

Father McCanny was also able to baptise K for me. He arranged the ceremony with the agreement of social services and the foster parents. I was very grateful; it was very important to me. We agreed on a small, private ceremony. X and his family somehow found out about it and turned up, uninvited. He hadn't seen his children for weeks. Some of the family were determined to tell me what they thought of me to my face. My barring order didn't extend to the church. I tried not to let it spoil the day.

That spring I began, slowly, to emerge back into the world. Carmel's office got in touch. The police wanted to interview me again. It had taken four months for them to complete their investigations. Carmel herself was still on maternity leave but I trusted her team.

In March 2003, I was back at Strand Road police station. I was interviewed by two detectives from the CID. The solicitor who was covering Carmel's maternity leave had already told me that it was his professional duty to remind clients that if they pleaded guilty at the first opportunity, they would be treated more favourably by the courts. I rejected this. I was innocent. He told me the police would make the same suggestions.

The detectives made it clear from the start that they thought I knew much more about what had happened to K than I was admitting; and that they viewed me as the most likely suspect. The questions were the same as those I had answered back in November. Going back over the twenty-four hours before K was taken to hospital, describing whom we'd been with, what we'd done. Who'd been alone with the baby. I appreciate that they had a job to do. They were, as one detective told me, 'only trying to get to the bottom of it'. But they were blunt.

'We've spoken to every doctor, every surgeon, that worked on K,' one police officer said, 'and every single one of them is saying that it was assault, that is, non-accidental, in their opinion. Now, these are all experts in what they're doing and we would take their opinion and rate it very highly indeed.'

They had not, in fact, spoken to 'every single medical expert'. But how was I to know they hadn't? And there was no mention of the word 'cancer', one diagnosis that had been put to me in the early days and which had so frightened me.

The police officer went on: 'You know we have to find out what happened to that child, and all the evidence we see is pointing at you.'

'No, I never touched the baby,' I protested. 'I wouldn't hurt [K], the child means too much to me.'

But no one was listening. I was the prime, in fact the only, suspect. I was informed that the police believed I had 'a case to answer' and it would be referred to the Director of Public Prosecutions. In plain and simple terms, they thought I was not being truthful and I was to stand trial for assaulting my baby.

Then it was back to going over the events of the day K was admitted to hospital. Was there anything else I could remember? Had anything come back to me?

No, it hadn't.

How was K?

I told them. K was six months old and getting chubby. K's health was being monitored but there had been no recurrence of the illness. K had only 10 per cent function in one kidney. I'd been told people can function with one kidney, but this still worried me. I added that K was a really happy, contented baby, and according to the foster mother, the baby had been like that 'from day one'. Thinking of K in the foster home only made me more vulnerable to what he asked next.

'Has K ever been dropped accidentally?'

'No,' I assured him.

'Right, you're sure of that?'

'Not by me.'

'To your knowledge, by anybody?' the officer pressed.

'No.'

'That's been discounted, OK.' He mentally ticked it off. 'Has an adult fallen on top of K at any stage?'

'No,' I replied.

'Again, by accident?'

'No,' I insisted.

The detective then referred to a new medical report. He told me it was written by a consultant surgeon, Dr E, who was 'one of the top men in Northern Ireland. Specifically in the paediatric department'. He was 'an expert', he repeated, listing his credentials as though they made him infallible.

Dr E, the detective assured me, had looked at 'all' the scans, talked to 'all' the other surgeons, seen 'all' the X-rays.

Again, how was I to know, back then, that he had not?

The detective did not read directly from Dr E's report. He never showed it to me. He just referred to it. He told me there was a 'large mass inside the abdomen'. The chances of this being caused non-accidentally were, he said, negligible. Then he told me what else the report said. The injury was to the left kidney and the spleen. The most likely cause was direct force, by something that hadn't penetrated the skin. He began to explain this in very simplistic terms. He told me the doctor's report suggested that there had been more than one blow to the lower left-hand side of K's stomach. He didn't think little J would have been strong enough to do this. Had K been dropped? he asked again.

I shook my head.

Some people, the detective suggested, might have a sense of guilt about this. They might feel that, even if it had happened accidentally, they were a 'bad parent'.

Was he hoping I'd put up my hands and admit that there'd been a dreadful accident? But there hadn't. I told him the truth.

'No.'

His mood changed.

'We believe you know more than you have told us. That you are covering up.'

'No.'

He'd been questioning me for more than four hours. I was drained. I had nothing more to say. The detective closed the file.

Once again, I was released on bail. The same, hypothetical five hundred pounds. My solicitor walked back with me through the gates, just as Carmel and I had done in November. Late autumn had turned to early spring and nothing had changed. The police still thought I had harmed my baby, they had made that clear enough. I knew for certain that I would go on trial for nearly killing my tiny, helpless child. There was nothing anyone could do to stop the Prosecution taking its course. It wasn't a case of whether I would go to court, but when.

It was about the same time that one couple who lived nearby began talking to me. Just a few words, just small talk, but I noticed that every time I came out the door they seemed to make a point of bumping into me. Then, one day, Jean asked me in for a cup of tea. It was so long since anyone had done that, I was overwhelmed by such a simple gesture of kindness.

Gradually, we got talking. Jean and her husband, Colum, knew about what had happened. They weren't interested in judging me. They were worried that they never saw me out and about, and that I'd lost so much weight. Jean knew I hadn't been looking after myself. She made it clear, from the start, that she'd heard all sorts of rumour and gossip about me, but she paid no heed to it. She knew the source and she didn't have any time for it. She insisted that I must come in for my dinner. They had four children of their own, three boys and a little girl. The youngest was almost exactly the same age as J. I couldn't help thinking they would have had such a good time playing together.

One evening, over dinner, the floodgates opened and through tears I told them the whole story. I must have covered fifteen years that night. They listened, without making any comments, just letting me talk. It was such a relief. I talked to my children in England every week, but I had no one to talk to like this. At the end of it all, they said they believed me. This meant so much. They knew Father McCanny and knew he believed me, too. They believed that a terrible injustice had been done.

From then on, hardly a day passed without us spending some time together. I'd pass on every little detail about my access meetings, how I'd see changes in J and K every week. My frustration at not being able to bring them home to play with their own toys in their own house. The pain of separation at the end of each visit, that never got any easier. But I was eating better and taking more care over my appearance. It was warmer and I'd go out for a long walk most days, more often than not to Carnhill, where I'd find my refuge in the chapel.

Jean's father, Johnnie, used to visit them a lot and we got to know each other quite well. One night when we were talking about the church, he asked me to come to a prayer group he was involved with, in the Bogside area of the city. He told me it was run by an Englishwoman, Adele, and her husband, Frankie. He was a Derryman and she'd come back to Ireland with him. Johnnie told me that people came to the group for all sorts of reasons, but they all supported each other. Some of them were recovering alcoholics or drug users who'd been sober and clean for as long as twenty years.

When I turned up that first Thursday night, Adele, a woman about fifteen years my senior, told me I looked 'just like a lifeless rag doll'. (And I had thought I was starting to get better.) The group welcomed me. Most of them had been through their own troubles and they took time to listen to mine. Afterwards, people came up to me to give me a hug, shake my hand, or to reassure me that everything would be all right in the end. I felt safe and surrounded by love and understanding. I told them that my father was Catholic but we hadn't been brought up in any religious tradition. Religious Education had been my favourite subject at school but no one had encouraged me to study it or to go to church. I told them about how my faith had grown since I'd come to Ireland, and how I'd felt it was important to have the children baptised as Catholics. I told them about the woman who had given me the prayer card to Saint Teresa. I still carried it everywhere with me. I told them about the hours I sat praying in Carnhill chapel. Adele thought it was amazing that someone like me – she called me a non-Catholic – had been drawn to sit and pray right beside the Blessed Sacrament. They encouraged my faith. It was very different from what I was used to in England, where religion didn't seem to be important in most people's lives.

Adele and I got on really well from the start. She has never lost her English accent – or her amusement at some of the goings-on in her adopted city. We'd share a laugh about being 'blow-ins'. It was as if someone had thrown me a lifeline and I really looked forward to Thursday nights.

Bit by bit, that summer, I was starting to get my life back on track. I still saw the children three times a week, in the same community centre. J, who would be three next birthday, was a bright child who was starting to ask questions about Mummy Louise and why she went away. J and I had had a very close bond before the child went into care; for long periods of time there'd just been the two of us, and J never lost that sense of our special relationship. We had had time to bond. K had spent much more of the first year with the foster family than with me, and I wondered if we would ever be able to reclaim those lost months. But I couldn't dwell on that. I concentrated on making each visit as special as I could, with a story or an improvised game. It would have been great to take them outdoors, but we stayed in the same cheerless room, time after time.

I hoped to be able to go to Northampton to see my older children and I was saving up for the flight; I couldn't let a year go past without seeing them. I was struggling to keep the relationships with my older children alive, too. Jake was at school; Jaz, Nina and Ayshea were growing up fast. At such a distance we found it hard to explain to each other what our everyday lives were like.

Carmel had had a daughter and returned from maternity leave in March. The new court session opened in September, and I'd been told that nothing would happen over the summer months, but that things would then move quickly. Jean and Colum were always there to lend a hand or offer a shoulder to cry on. My moods were still all over the place. I'd be excited about seeing J and K; then, after a visit, I'd be frustrated, or angry, or tearful, or despairing. I had to put on a brave front for J but I couldn't keep it up all the time. There was so much I wanted to share with the children, but I couldn't. Even a walk to the park or a turn on the swings would have meant a lot.

Colum and Jean involved me in all their special occasions. I was at every birthday party, decorating the rooms, making cards, playing party games, baking and icing cakes. But nothing could mask the fact that I should be doing this for J and K. I knew I couldn't be there on their birthdays. I was their mother and I was excluded.

Carmel and I met up in September. The police investigation was almost completed and she understood that the Foyle Trust would be asking for me to be assessed as part of their case. Carmel also told me she had arranged junior counsel to represent me in court, Michael McAleer BL, and was to confirm a senior counsel to lead the case. She expected I'd be granted legal aid for two barristers because the charges against me would be serious.

On 21 October, Carmel arranged for me to come to her office, where the police formally charged me with causing grievous bodily harm with intent to baby K. I was returned to the local court to be charged in front of a magistrate. It wasn't a surprise, but hearing that I was actually going to appear in a public court sent a chill through me. Carmel had been very straight with me and I respected her for it. If I was convicted, I was facing a long jail sentence. The maximum was ten years. A guilty verdict would end all contact with J and K, who would almost definitely be put up for adoption, and any contact with my other children would only be permitted under supervision.

As I sat shaking in the office afterwards and she plied me with strong coffee, Carmel also warned me that the police press office would confirm to the media that I had been charged. From this point on, journalists would be free to contact the court service to see when I was due to appear. My case would then be reported in the papers. On 31 October 2003, the Friday edition of the *Derry Journal*, the local paper with the largest circulation, carried the story on page six:

> A 34 year old Derry woman has been returned for trial to the City's Crown Court in relation to an incident last year. Louise Mason, of 3 Ferndale Drive, is charged that on a date unknown between October 17–20, 2002, she caused grievous bodily harm to another person, with the intention of causing such harm ...

The very thing I had been dreading was now coming to pass. The Family Court hearing was set for January 2004. The trial date was set for 20 May, but Judge Finnegan was to adjourn it because one of the key medical witnesses was abroad. A new date was to be set for after 10 June, but the summer recess was to come and go and it would be more than a year before the trial would get underway in November 2004.

The Family Court

The winter of 2003 was busy, and how I appreciated that. Carmel and I were working together, preparing for the two court cases that would decide the children's future, and mine. There was the criminal trial, which would be held at Londonderry Crown Court, where a jury would decide whether I was guilty of causing grievous bodily harm with intent to K. Then there was the case in the Family Division of the High Court in Belfast. It was to hear the Foyle Trust's application for a long-term care order for J and K.

Carmel kept me informed about what was likely to be put as evidence against me. I know every solicitor has a professional duty to do their best for their clients but I felt then, and now, that the bond between us is more than a working arrangement. Carmel was always prepared to go the extra mile to help me. And she always told me the truth, even when she knew it would hurt. She warned me that the medical evidence would do us no favours and would be nearly impossible to contest. Judge and juries naturally respect doctors as knowledgeable people who tell the truth about medical matters which the rest of us don't understand. They are believed. And the medical evidence was that K had been seriously assaulted. The circumstantial evidence was that I was the only real suspect.

Carmel also explained to me how the Family Courts work. They are used to decide issues like custody, and whether children can be taken abroad. They also deal with vulnerable adults and they hear cases from people who have, say, been detained against their wishes in psychiatric hospital.

I'd won my child custody case when I moved to Northern Ireland – no one had ever suggested I had been anything other than a good mother – but I'd lost out because the court had refused to allow me to take the children to live in Ireland. So I knew that a family hearing would mean reports from health visitors and social workers, and statements from the adults and older children who were involved. The case in Belfast was on a much bigger scale than the one in Northampton because it would involve the care of the children until they were eighteen and was between the Trust and me, not between two parents. This meant the court might have to consider freeing the children for adoption.

Family Courts are usually held in the same building as Criminal Courts, but behind closed doors. Their business is carried out in private. There are no juries. The judge makes the decision. There's no public gallery for supporters and friends, and reporters aren't allowed to write about their business, except in very special circumstances. Even inside the closed court, witnesses are often referred to only by an initial or a pseudonym, to try to ensure their anonymity. It's only thanks to a ruling by Judge Gillen in February 2008 that I can write about my case at all. It's also against the law to talk about Family Court cases. I've often been asked why I didn't go to my MP, my MLA, a lobby group or the press for help. The simple answer is that if I had, I'd have been in contempt of court and could have been jailed for it. And Family Court proceedings become active from the minute children are taken into care.

Another big difference between family and criminal cases is that in a criminal case the jury must be convinced beyond reasonable doubt that the person on trial has committed the crime. The defendant doesn't have to prove their innocence. Family Courts, on the other hand, make their decisions on the balance of probability. They make decisions based on a social worker's or a doctor's opinion, or feeling, or instinct. There's less emphasis on circumstantial evidence or on hard facts. I thought then, and still do, that this makes them very biased in favour of the professional witnesses. Their word is taken as the truth.

I was still allowed to see J and K three times a week. J was getting so grown up, and was at playschool, meeting other children. We taught each other little rhymes and verses. Stories were always popular and dressing up was a big hit. I'd lend J my own jacket and shoes and we'd drape them round the child in different ways. I might have a scarf or a hat with me. The community centre had no dressing-up box and very few books. Sometimes, I was allowed to bring things on my access visits. Crayons and paper, to draw on. There were no educational toys there. Budgets were tight.

K was a toddler now, full of energy, who bonded with me as a friendly adult and did not recognise me in any maternal sense. J knew me as Mummy Louise and was closer to me. I felt that J was finding the whole situation very confusing. When I was depressed, I'd wonder if it wouldn't be better for J not to see me at all than to have Mummy Louise appearing and disappearing for no reason that the child could understand. It was just too unsettling. But I'd give myself a good talking to and remind myself that if things went in our favour, both children could be back with me before 2004 was over.

Carmel had explained that when the Trust was preparing its case for the long-term care order, it would be contacting both Sol and Trevor to ask them for their version of why I had gone to Ireland and would ask Sol why he had gone to court to stop me taking his children with me. Trevor was unhappy about the way my life had turned out and resented the involvement of the social services, but he always co-operated with me and let me see Jake without any hassle. At six, Jake was a happy, well-balanced child who looked forward to seeing me but who was very close to his father.

I needed a lot of emotional support and that came from Jean and Colum and my friends in the prayer group. They were a tower of strength. We laughed and cried, talked and prayed together. They must have been worn out telling me that everything would be all right in the end.

Carmel had been granted legal aid for two barristers to represent me in the Family Court. I'd met the junior, Michael McAleer, who, like Carmel, was down to earth and pulled no punches. She'd secured a woman barrister to lead him as my senior counsel. They had a positive approach – no legal team goes to court to lose – but I knew they were preparing me for the fact that we would probably lose.

I suspected my psychiatric report would go against us. The year before, when I was at my lowest, the Trust had referred me to one of their leading clinical psychologists, Dr F. He is often asked by the Trust and the police to prepare court reports. I had two one-hour sessions with him in Derry, in April and May 2003. It seemed a very short amount of time for him to assess my personality, but it was all I got. The sessions hadn't gone well. I found Dr F unsympathetic. It may be my impression but I felt he didn't really listen to what I was saying before he moved on to the next question.

My legal team had seen the social workers' reports, which stated that they thought adoption was in the best interests of the children. J and K had been fortunate to be placed together in a foster family, and to stay with the same family most of the time they'd been in care. (J had been in a short-term placement until K was also fostered.) But the Trust wanted them to have the security of adoption. To know they would live with the same family until they were eighteen. It would also mean they could change their name to get rid of any links with the mother who had harmed K.

Dr F recommended me for therapeutic family work and I was later referred to an independent health consultant, ML. We hit it off straightaway. I really enjoyed my six sessions with her, between September and December 2003. We talked about my parenting skills and bringing up children on my own. She was reassuring, telling me she thought I was a good mother, and she reminded me that the health visitors' reports on J and K had been very positive. They'd described both children as being well cared for and loved. I was sorry when these sessions came to an end. I'd learned more about myself and how I related to my children. They gave me confidence in my ability to be a good parent.

The case was held at the Family Division of the High Court in Chichester Street in Belfast, with Judge McLaughlin presiding. It was to open in January 2004, and was expected to last two weeks. Then disaster struck. My senior counsel suddenly withdrew from the case because of professional commitments. She was legally entitled to do so, but at such short notice it left Carmel with a big problem. I could sense Carmel's concern. How would she be able to find, never mind instruct, a replacement barrister in a matter of days? She engaged Ken McMahon QC, who is better known for his Prosecution work. He was on holiday with his family but undertook to read my case notes as soon as he returned.

On the opening day, I was terrified. I hadn't slept the night before. I knew people were praying for me, but Carmel's expression told me we'd need all the prayers we could get. The Foyle Trust had five doctors lined up to give evidence. We had no one. I looked round the courtroom at the faces of my current social work team and felt so angry that they had the right to take my children away when I'd done nothing wrong. There were four or five of them in court, but over the last year I must have had dozens, all following the same policy. Why? I had no criminal convictions. They'd had access to my medical records and had been unable to find anything there that would make me an unfit mother. I had no history of alcohol or drug problems, or psychiatric illness. Instead, they were prepared to judge me on my past; that I had left four children in England to move to Derry.

I knew I wouldn't get the chance to put my side of the story until I was cross-examined; and that would be after they'd had several days to put their case to the judge. I had my regrets about going to Derry. Not the move itself, but my naivety. I had never imagined that Sol would try to stop me; after all, he wasn't involved in his children's lives at that time. I could not have foreseen that my mother would become depressed and suddenly decide to hand over Jaz and Nina to their father, especially without talking to me about it first. Sol's and mine had always been a stormy relationship and I can only imagine that he and his new wife resented having their lives disrupted by the unexpected arrival of two teenagers, whom he'd hardly seen for two years. And so he was going to stop me getting what I wanted, which was to move them to Ireland. He could be that vindictive. Yes, I had my regrets, but I couldn't put the clock back.

I am prohibited by law from describing what happened in the Family Court. I cannot give any account of what was said or details of any of the witnesses or their statements. The only information I am permitted to provide – and this only because of a relaxation of restrictions on publicity by Judge Gillen – is that the hearing took place because Foyle Trust had applied for a care order in respect of J and K. During those proceedings the meaning of a care order application was explained to me. I understood this to mean that an order could be granted if the child concerned is suffering or is likely to suffer significant harm and that the harm must be attributable to the care given or likely to given by a parent. In assessing this, the standard of proof considered by the court was on the balance of probabilities.

The hearing lasted for two weeks and I found them incredibly difficult and traumatic. Every day, Carmel drove me to and from the court, a round trip of about four hours. On the way there she would go over what was expected to happen that day; who would be giving evidence; and what they were likely to say. On the way home, we'd go over the day's events and discuss how it had gone for us. Usually, not so good. Then we'd chat about Carmel's family, or my children, slipping in and out of our personal lives and professional business. I was missing out on six sessions with J and K because of the court hearing. It would be worth it, if we won. We never mentioned what would happen if we lost. We were tired every morning, heading up the M2 to Belfast, and worn out every night. We were living on coffee and sandwiches.

At the end of the second week Judge McLaughlin brought the hearing to a close. Carmel said it would be another few weeks before he publicly announced whether he'd granted the Trust's application for a long-term care order.

In the meantime, however, the Trust seemed confident that it had proved its case. The care order would remain in place. My access was cut back to two visits a week, each lasting for an hour and a half. This was clearly meant to prepare J and K, and me, for the time when the Trust would have the judge's ruling on its side and access would be stopped for good. My children were slipping away from me and there was nothing I could do.

Carmel attended the Family Court on 1 April 2004 to hear the judge read out his ruling, and as soon as I spoke to her and read the judgment for myself, I was in despair. The judge had granted the Trust application for a care order and had ruled that on the balance of probability my baby had suffered a non-accidental injury and the injury was probably caused by me. I was devastated. I still didn't understand how baby K had become so sick. I'd been told the baby might have cancer. Had that been a misdiagnosis? Or were the doctors who thought K had received a blow to the kidney the ones who were wrong? If it was 100 per cent definite that K had been assaulted, and I knew I hadn't done it, then who had?

The Trust thought the outcome of the criminal trial was a foregone conclusion. The trial would be a formality. I would be convicted and go to prison for anything up to ten years. J and K would be adopted and grow up with a new identity. All they'd know about their birth mother would be that she'd been responsible for deliberately and seriously injuring her baby. In those circumstances, why would they want to trace me when they were adults?

Carmel did her best to comfort me. She kept saying we'd expected as much. All through the hearing, we'd known things hadn't gone well for us. There was no denying the power of the medical evidence. At least, Carmel reminded me, the judgment wouldn't be made public. There'd be nothing in the papers about it. And at least the children hadn't been freed for adoption. Carmel didn't say the word 'yet'. She didn't need to. It hung in the air. Put it behind you, she urged and we'll do our best at the criminal trial. That's all we can do.

We both knew the odds were stacked against us. We had no medical evidence to back our case. Apart from a handful of loyal friends, what did we have? Only the truth.

Living in Limbo

It was now the summer of 2004. Once Judge McLaughlin had made his ruling my access was cut back to once a week; then, in order to prepare the children for adoption, to one visit a fortnight. And now the Trust was telling me I would only be allowed to see J and K for an hour and a half once a month. How can you explain that to children who are not yet two and four? One of whom has never had a chance to bond with you? J still clung to me at every visit and cried after me when I left, but I tried to reassure myself that children are adaptable and that their foster home was a loving one. I had to, or I would have cracked.

An hour and a half per month is such a ridiculously short time. The implication was obvious – the Trust was easing J and K into a situation where they wouldn't see me again, ever. I tried not to think about that. If I had, I wouldn't have been able to cope – the thought of it would have taken away my will to keep fighting.

I'd never had a Christmas with K. My last one with J was in 2001, when J was almost a year old. Birthdays were the same. I'd never been with K on a birthday and hadn't spent one with J since 2002. They had to be 'celebrated' with me on the nearest available access visit. I'd bring their gift and card, and we'd sing 'Happy Birthday'. That was it.

As a little family, we were missing out on all the milestones. Not only did I miss out on the special occasions, I'd never done things with J and K together – never. I'd never taken them both to the park, or swimming. I'd never bought them both an ice cream. I'd never read K a bedtime story. Little things that we take for granted. Instead, my only contact with them was in that dreary, functional room in the community centre with no real play facilities and a social worker monitoring my every move.

Jean and Colum knew that the access visits were what kept me going and they were concerned that with these reduced to a mere token, I'd retreat back under the duvet as I had done during those eight awful months in the winter of 2002–3. They told me I had to be strong. I had to use this extra spare time to build the best possible life for the day when we were all back together. A broken mother was no use to her children. Summer was here and they encouraged me to get out of the house as much as possible.

Up until July, I was in and out of the town with Carmel, getting briefed for the Criminal Court. Then there were my long walks to Carnhill, to the church. I'd think things out as I walked through the different estates that are scattered over the west bank of the city. Exercise, fresh air, green spaces, talking to Jean and Colum, phone calls to the children in Northampton, the Thursday night prayer group and a sense of routine helped me keep my sanity.

July came; a quiet time in the courts. The Magistrates' Court, which deals with less serious offences, continues to sit for most of July and August. My trial, however, would be held in the Crown Court, which doesn't sit over the summer months. Carmel told me there would be a backlog of cases in September – there always is – and these would be dealt with before my trial, which was looking like it could be in October or even November.

If I was seeing very little of J and K, I was seeing nothing at all of my children back in England. I tried to stay in touch by phone as much as possible, and I loved hearing all about their plans. Jaz and Nina would be fifteen and fourteen that winter. Jaz was hopeful of getting into sixth form, while Nina was going to leave school after GCSEs. Ayshea was now almost thirteen and Jake was seven, and all of them wished they could have spent time with J and K. I tried to make the best of things but the phone calls never seemed enough – it was heartbreaking not being able to spend time with them.

Ayshea was finding life with Sol difficult and told me that Nina, in particular, was clashing with him. I knew Nina's strong-mindedness wouldn't go down well with

Sol, who is a very controlling person. Ayshea was getting more like her big sister in temperament and I could see that as the girls got older and their own personalities developed there would be more and more clashes of will with their father.

Jaz talked about a trip he'd made Libya to stay with the family for a couple of weeks. He was always very welcome there and his Libyan relatives spoiled him with kindness. But he told me that when he came back home, he felt certain that his future was in England. He found the way of life in Libya too different from what he'd grown up with.

I was glad that Jaz, Nina and Ayshea were all enjoying spending time with my parents. Maybe, in time, my rift with my parents would heal. We kept in touch through the children and I phoned Mum from time to time to keep her and Dad up to date with what was happening. All four children really missed J. They remembered J as a lovely baby, who had disappeared from their lives. I felt really sad about that. They'd never got to know K, but they were mature enough to sense how much I'd been hurt.

I thought about looking for a job, to keep busy and to boost my self-esteem. But it wouldn't have been realistic to try to come off benefit payments. I was receiving legal aid for my case. Friends introduced me to their friends and my circle of acquaintances grew. One such friend-of-a-friend was John. He was on his own and lived and worked near the city centre. We met in July 2004 and got on well. I agreed to go out with him, even though the last thing I was looking for was a serious relationship. On our third date, I told him all about my children, the older ones in England and also about J and K being in foster care. I told him about the Family Court case and how I was waiting to go on trial for assaulting K. I told him the facts and I also told him how it made me feel. How it had destroyed my life, and left me with no confidence. How I felt low a lot of the time. How hard it was to keep fighting and to stay convinced that it would all work out. John was a good and empathic listener. He didn't interrupt me or pass any comments. When I was finished, he promised to do anything he could to help me.

Nevertheless, I honestly didn't expect to see him again. Why would a single working man want to be burdened with all this? I told myself that he'd have a good think about it and disappear. I was wrong. He told his family all about it. His sister, Sally, was horrified at my story and got in touch – she, too, offered to help me and became a good friend, independent of John.

John and I talked through a lot of things. I decided the time was right to move away from Fernabbey. I felt strong enough. It meant moving away from Jean and Colum, but I intended to stay within walking distance and they knew I would keep up our friendship. My house was too big for a woman on her own. I'd been hanging on to the tenancy hoping the children would soon be back. That was obviously going to take time and I knew that when they were with me again, the Housing Executive would find us a family home in a matter of weeks.

Ferndale Drive had too many bad memories. As they had got to know me well, people in the prayer group had started to tell me what they'd heard said about me in the past. Allegations that I hadn't fed my children properly. That I had left them alone in the house. Malicious rumours spread by malicious people who didn't even know me, and which had no truth in them whatsoever. I know that the people who told me these things were just warning me who my enemies were. I felt hurt and a bit frightened. Did people who had never met me believe these rumours? Dirt sticks, and it sticks for a long time. I will never know how many of my social workers had heard things like this and may have been influenced by them.

So I wanted to move on. I wanted to be free of all the negative feelings associated with the place, free to make a new start with J and K when I did get them back. True, it was a link with a happier past also, when J and K were with me. But K wouldn't remember the house and J probably wouldn't, either. I looked round for a place in the city centre, which would be handy for going to and from Carmel's office and the court. It would also be nearer the prayer group. And, while I had had no contact with them since the christening, it would take me further away from X's extended family. I found a small flat owned by a private landlord. It would be easy to heat and look after, and, once I'd given up my tenancy, my housing benefit covered the rent.

In September, Carmel began taking me through my criminal trial, step by step. I went to the Crown Court in Bishop Street just to get a sense of what the courtroom looked like. At least we wouldn't have to travel to and from Belfast. I knew that it would be more formal than the Family Court, but also more open to the public. The barristers and judge would wear wigs and gowns. There was a large public gallery behind the dock and, to the right, was the press bench with room for about six reporters. Carmel told me that sometimes there would be no one there to report on what was going on. A big case, or one with some sort of particular news interest, might attract a steady two or three. The jury would sit on the two benches on the left. The witness box was up a small flight of steps on the right-hand side. The legal teams sat in front of the dock, separated from the person on trial by a Perspex screen. I was told that this was a fairly new addition to the courtroom furnishings. One reason it had been put up was to protect the person on trial from members of the public.

I'd have the same legal team as before. This was good news. Very often barristers who specialise in family cases don't do criminal work, and vice versa. Also, experienced and successful barristers are very much in demand and may have to be booked well in advance. We hadn't got a definite trial date. And while I was grateful to have legal aid, it's not the best paid work for a top lawyer. I'm sure both Michael McAleer and Ken McMahon could have commanded much larger fees elsewhere. Having the same team made me more confident, as we'd got to know each other as people.

Carmel would be sitting right in front of me, she promised, in case she had to convey messages to and from my barristers. I was to try to let her know if I ever felt I needed a break in giving evidence. We could adjourn to the coffee bar on the ground floor of the building.

We got a court date for early November and Carmel told me she was confident the trial would go ahead. A few days before, she sat me down with Michael and Ken to discuss our options. Ken told me, as tactfully and as gently as he could, that it was his duty in law to remind me, again, that I still had the option of pleading guilty. I faced two charges – of causing grievous bodily harm with intent, and the lesser charge of causing grievous bodily harm. The lesser charge meant that I hadn't intended to hurt the baby. He told me the judge had a legal obligation to give favourable treatment to a defendant who pleaded guilty before the trial started. It saved the courts time and money. It spared witnesses the trauma of appearing in court. A guilty plea might mean that I faced only the lesser charge. This would mean a shorter sentence – maybe as little as two years – and the statutory authorities would help me to come to terms with it. I'd have the support of probation, counselling services …

'No,' I insisted. I was innocent and I was determined to have the opportunity to tell the judge and jury under oath that I had not harmed my baby. I could only do my best to make them believe me.

On the morning of Tuesday, 9 November 2004, Ken, Michael, Carmel and I walked together through the security check at the entrance to the courthouse. Some local newspapers had already reported 'a thirty-six-year-old woman was to go on trial later today charged with causing grievous bodily harm with intent to her four-week-old infant'. (I was actually thirty-five at the time.) There were crowds of people on the steps, around the entrance and in the coffee area on the ground floor. I felt all eyes were on me. I was sick with fright. No one needed to remind me that this was my last chance. No one needed to remind me that if I lost, I was facing anything up to ten years in jail and I would lose my children forever.

I hadn't agonised about what to wear because I didn't have a big choice. Like Carmel, I opted for a dark trouser suit. I wanted to look clean, tidy and respectable. I breathed deeply and walked up the steps, through the doors into the court building. People were bustling around, coming and going, solicitors were being paged, policemen lining the entrances to the different courts, children crying. I hadn't expected people would have children with them. I stood beside Carmel, looking round me, clutching the prayer card in my pocket. I caught sight of John's sister, Sally, and smiled. John was at work and I hadn't wanted him there anyway, so we'd agreed Sally would be there, every day, for support.

Carmel looked at her watch. It was ten o'clock. The court was to open at half past. She led me down a long corridor, through a heavy door and up two flights of stone stairs to the landing. Ahead of me was the entrance to Court Four.

The Crown Court

I have no idea how many prayers were being said for me that Tuesday morning when the Prosecution opened the case against me. We sat and waited while the members of the public and the witnesses filed in and filled the benches at the back. I saw Janice and Peter, and several members of X's family. I looked away. Then I identified the two female police officers from the Care Unit at Maydown who'd interviewed me back at the start. They sat to the right of the dock, near the press bench. They were there for the Prosecution.

Reporters started to take their place on the press bench. Carmel whispered their names, or who they worked for. The local papers, of course – the *Derry Journal* and the *Belfast Telegraph*. The BBC and UTV. The *Irish News*. Carmel had explained that some reporters were freelance and would be reporting for a number of different outlets. One reporter there worked for Downtown and the Independent Radio News outlet. He also supplied reports to the Dublin papers and the English tabloids. The BBC would cover radio and television for the Derry area, for Northern Ireland, and for the national network. It would also send material to the Republic's state broadcasters, RTÉ. Another man was identified to me as being from the Press Agency, which makes its court reports available worldwide. I couldn't believe there was so much interest in my case. I knew they were looking over at me as they got out their notebooks and checked to make sure their mobile phones were switched off. What were they thinking? Did I look like a woman who would harm her baby and then lie to cover up?

Half past ten came and went. I looked round anxiously towards the door in front of me, on the left, where the judge would come in. A man in a black gown stood beside it. Carmel had explained he was the tipstaff, who would tell us when to stand up and when the court was officially in session. The clerk, a smartly dressed woman of about forty, was already seated at the judge's bench, which is up a short flight of steps at the front of the court. Spread in front of her were piles and piles of papers and files. Each of them must have been a foot deep.

'Silence in court. All rise.'

We rose in unison as the tipstaff announced the arrival of the imposing figure of the Londonderry Recorder, Judge Philpott, QC. She walked in purposefully, her robes flowing behind her, her white rolled wig covering most of her short dark hair.

'This Crown Court now stands open.'

Two prison officers summoned me over to the dock. I stepped in, trying to look more composed than I felt. The atmosphere was tense. Reporters shuffled and coughed, craning their necks to get a good look at me. I knew that every single person in that courtroom would be studying me; those who didn't know me would be scrutinising me for the smallest details in my appearance and demeanour that might give them a clue about the sort of person standing trial. What impression did I give? Apart from abject fear?

I was ordered to stand, flanked by the two prison officers. The clerk rose, papers in hand.

'Louise Jane Mason, are you ready for your trial?'

I nodded.

'Louise Jane Mason you are charged …'

She read both charges in their full form, in the complicated language of the law. The reporters scribbled furiously. I felt the eyes of the public gallery on my back. I imagined them thinking, this is her, the woman who battered her baby. That's what she looks like. In theory, of course, we are all innocent until proven guilty. But I knew there were those in the courtroom who had prejudged me, condemned me before I even opened my mouth.

The DPP's senior counsel, Liam McCollum, QC, opened the case for the Prosecution.

I went over Carmel's instructions in my head. She had explained that this was when he would address the jury and tell them why he thought they should find me guilty. My legal team wouldn't get the chance to speak until the Prosecution had finished their case. That could be in a week's time.

Mr McCollum told the court there was 'evidence to show the woman had assaulted [K] and the baby had suffered serious injuries to the kidney as a result'. He then said that apart from 'three brief occasions', I had been alone with the baby during the twelve-hour period when the injuries were most probably sustained. I knew this period had varied from twenty-four hours to twelve hours, to six, to as little as two.

Mr McCollum traced the events of the night and day before K was admitted to hospital. It was all so familiar to me but not to the jury. I looked over at the jury benches. Nine women and three men. Would women be more sympathetic or would they be more ready to condemn me? I made myself look down at my hands, or straight ahead. It was pointless to try to gauge their reaction. The story continued. The night out. My taxi ride to the Post Office the next day. Peter's visit. The trip to the shop for milk. Calling over to Janice's. Her driving us to the Waterside Health Centre and then to hospital. My very sick baby K.

'The mother has offered no explanation in police interviews as to how the baby was injured,' Mr McCollum told the court.

This was true. Because I didn't have one. The Prosecution said that K had been assaulted and that only only four people who could have done this – me, and three others. Could Peter have done it when he called at my house to apologise about the night out? He had been alone with K for a brief time. Or could it have been the taxi driver, that morning, when I'd left K in the taxi as I nipped in to the shop? Finally – was there a possibility that my toddler J could have been responsible? But these were rhetorical questions only. The Prosecution said none of the other three could have harmed K. J wouldn't have been strong enough; the taxi driver had only been alone with K for a very short time and even then in full view of passers-by; Peter, too, had only been with K a short time, and had been minding J as well. None had a motive. I knew I hadn't done it. But I had no logical explanation for K's injury. The Prosecution didn't mention the possibility of cancer, or neuroblastoma. What explanation had I to offer the police when I didn't have one for myself?

Then it was the turn of the medical witnesses. Their evidence was so hard to listen to. It went into detail about K's appalling condition when first admitted to the Accident and Emergency department at Altnagelvin Hospital, two years ago. It was heartbreaking to listen to, conjuring up, as it did, the graphic image of this tiny baby, fighting for life. Witnesses, in turn, described how my how my 'lovely little baby', who was obviously well cared for, was suddenly in 'immediate danger of death' when examined in hospital two years ago. How the baby was listless, pale and had a temperature that could not be recorded. How internal bleeding was diagnosed, and resuscitation carried out. How the baby was admitted as an emergency, first to Altnagelvin Hospital and then to the Royal Belfast Hospital for Sick Children. No one could have failed to have been moved by their testimony.

The witnesses from Altnagelvin testified first. The registrar on call, Dr J, took the stand. She said the decision was taken to transfer baby K to Belfast because there was no consultant paediatric surgeon available in Derry. It was thought the baby might need surgery for internal bleeding. Dr J said that despite two transfusions, baby K's blood count was dropping because of an 'active bleed'. The doctor said that when she told me about the decision to transfer my baby to the Royal, I was 'very hard to talk to, as I appeared very withdrawn' and there were 'other people' around me. I could only remember Janice being there with me. Perhaps she meant the other people in the A & E unit. Dr J added that when told the bleeding was probably coming from a tumour, I had asked, 'Could it be anything other than a tumour?' She suggested this was an unusual thing to say.

Again, I would have thought it was the first thing any mother would ask if confronted with the sudden possibility that her child has cancer – could it be anything else? Is the child dying?

Another doctor from Altnagelvin, Dr M, described baby K as being lethargic, with a very low haemoglobin count, a low heart rate and severe anaemia. These, she said, could be signs of an infection or a cancer such as leukaemia.

'This baby was seriously ill,' she said. 'We were very concerned about this baby.'

The next medical witness to take the stand was Dr C. He confirmed he had been the duty surgeon at the Royal on the weekend of 18–20 October 2002. He said he discussed K's case with Dr B, the consultant paediatrician at Altnagelvin. Between them they had agreed K should be transferred to Belfast. The baby arrived there at 11 p.m. on Sunday 20th. Dr C gave details of the injury to the kidney area. He told the jury that the degree of force needed to sustain such an injury 'would be similar to the child falling from a first floor window or being involved in a car crash'.

I heard the ripple of reaction run through the courtroom. The press were writing it all down. I could hardly blame them. What sort of person could do that to a tiny baby?

Dr C added that, in his opinion, the injury was caused by a kick or blow to the kidney, or by an adult landing on one knee on the child. There was the possibility of someone tripping and landing on one knee on the baby. But when he had spoken to me about it, I could offer no explanation.

'It is difficult to imagine an accident causing it,' he went on, 'because most accidents would entail other injuries to the body such as lacerations or bruising ... for a kidney or spleen to be injured in this case it would need force to be directed straight on to those organs.'

I knew the medical evidence against me was strong. We are brought up to respect the medical profession. We think of doctors as people with authority. People who never make mistakes. Juries are ordinary people, like the rest of us. Our peers. One or two of them were visibly upset by what they were hearing.

We broke for coffee. Carmel was talking to Michael and Ken, but I wasn't taking anything in. I felt very vulnerable. I felt everyone was looking at me and passing judgement.

Janice was called after the break. She was described as a civilian witness who could not be identified to protect K's anonymity. (It had been suggested earlier that I should not be named publicly to protect K, despite the fact that my name had already been printed in newspapers across the country.)

Her evidence was factually accurate, but I wondered at her comments about my behaviour. She told the court that when the baby was admitted to hospital, I 'calmed down', but when she visited me there the next day she found I had 'no conversation' and was in a 'wee world of my own'.

Yet again I wondered how people expect a mother to behave when she is told her tiny child's life is in danger? It's an impossible situation. Who defines how a mother is expected to behave? If you struggle to keep calm, and hold things together, you're cold and callous; if you break down in tears, you're incapable and emotionally unstable. Either can be interpreted as a sign of guilt – if you choose to see it that way.

That was the end of the day's proceedings. Sally and a friend of hers came over to me to walk me home. They did their best to keep my spirits up. They hurried me past X's relatives. John called to see me later but I was numb. I felt totally helpless.

My trial made the headlines not just in the local Derry papers and press across Northern Ireland, but in the English papers as well. On one front page, in large type, was the headline: 'Mum on GBH trial. 4-week-old baby battered by Ulster woman.' I felt sick. Gutted. Carmel said this might only be in the Irish edition of the paper. My family in Northampton knew about the trial but I didn't want to bring trouble to their door with headlines like this.

DAY TWO

I walked into the courtroom the next day feeling the whole world was against me and waiting for me to get what people thought I deserved. In fact, I nearly didn't make it into court at all that Wednesday. The ladies' toilets outside Court Four were the setting for the unreported drama of the trial. I had been particularly upset to hear once again, from my supporters, that X's family were making the same unfounded allegations against me. They were approaching anyone who would listen to them. I locked myself in the toilet and lay down on the floor of the cubicle, sobbing to Carmel through the bolted door that I couldn't go on. I couldn't go into the dock. It was too much to bear. I was giving up. Carmel, positioned between the door and the washbasin, was delivering the pep talk of her life, in turn, cajoling and threatening. And in the narrow corridor outside, two gowned and wigged, distinguished gentlemen, excluded from this inner sanctum, querulously whispered to their instructing solicitor to tell them what on earth was going on? And could she please sort it out, quickly?

Later that day, in the same toilets, a woman reporter told one of my friends that the gossipmongers had been ringing up the papers to spread malicious rumours about me. When my friend filled me in, I was appalled by what people were saying. Their allegations were cruel and totally unfounded. But if the reporter had heard them who else had?

The day opened with the evidence of Dr K from the Royal. She told the court that she had first seen K two days after admission to the hospital and that the baby was 'well cared for, well nourished, clean and lovely'. There were 'no signs that K had not been cared for well'. The doctor said she could see swelling and a bluish discolouration on the left side of the abdomen.

'In my opinion there had been some trauma, some force used against the abdomen,' she added. 'A quite significant amount of force to produce the injuries which had occurred.'

Dr K went on to describe how she had taken personal

statements both from me, and from X, 'who has only seen K once, briefly, since the birth'. This was the only contribution he had made to the investigation – to make a statement for the social services confirming he was the father and explaining that he didn't have any contact with J and K, or me. The doctor added that 'X has three other children', and I had four, who lived with their fathers in England, as well as J, who had been living with me.

It was factual. But I could sense the disapproving glances from some jurors. I had no chance to explain the circumstances. I could imagine what they must be thinking. Six children, by three different men. And none of them living with me. Why?

There was nothing particularly newsworthy in her evidence. The press had to settle for 'Mum accused of assaulting baby'.

DAY THREE

On Thursday, it was back to going over the same medical evidence that had been haunting me for two years. As if I hadn't gone over it, time and again, trying to work out what could have happened to change my baby from a healthy happy infant to become, over the space of a few hours, a very sick baby struggling for survival. It made for emotive and painful listening. Again, we heard how K had been admitted as an emergency to Altnagelvin, and then to the Royal. Dr A, the GP who first examined the baby at the health centre, told the court he had decided 'within seconds' to admit K to hospital. He said K was 'obviously very unwell' and he was 'concerned' about the infant's pallor. Taking up the chronology, Dr B, who examined K on admission to Altnagelvin, said the child was 'extremely ill and in danger of death' if appropriate action was not taken immediately. Both doctors testified that they had initially diagnosed a tumour or blood disorder, such as leukaemia, causing internal bleeding, but accepted the eventual diagnosis by doctors at the Royal that K had sustained a non-accidental injury in the kidney area, delivered with considerable force, causing internal bleeding.

And it was on that note, after I had relived the trauma of the events of two years ago, that the judge adjourned for the weekend. She reminded the jury that they were forbidden to discuss the case with anyone.

What would they make of the evidence so far?

I went to the prayer group that night, and then stayed indoors over the weekend. I didn't want to talk to anyone. I didn't want to go to the shops and walk past the billboards with the news headlines. I started to feel a deep sense of despair.

WEEK TWO

There were fewer reporters in court the second week. Sally had got talking to one of them, who'd explained that they'd all be back for my evidence and for the summing-up and verdict. X's family were still there in force. So more of John's family started coming to court to support me. Jean came when she could. At first I hadn't wanted my friends to sit through the evidence. I didn't want them hearing the accusations that were being levelled at me. But now I began to appreciate them being there. The public gallery divided down the middle: X's family ranged against my supporters. I wished that my mum had been in touch to wish me well. I wished one of my family could have come over from Northampton. I didn't take it personally; as I've said, they're not really people to get involved (except when I moved to Derry). But it would have made a big difference to know that members of my family were in court, supporting me. At one stage, Deborah rang me and said she and Mum were thinking of coming over. I told them that would be great, and tried not to get too hopeful, as my instincts told me they wouldn't come. I was right. I don't think they understood how serious things were.

Peter gave his evidence on the Tuesday. He denied any involvement in injuring K. He told the court that he had come over to my house to apologise because my night out had been spoiled and that he had agreed to mind the children while I popped to the shop for milk. Perhaps most significantly, he told the jury that the minute he arrived at my door I'd told him K had been very unsettled. Implying that K was already ill – or had already been assaulted.

That day a reporter told my friends that X's family had been approaching members of the press, telling them that they'd be forgiving 'if only Louise would put her hands up and admit it'. That upset me. Most things did, that week.

On the Wednesday, it was my turn to give evidence. I left the dock, climbed in to the witness box and took the oath. Clutching my prayer card and looking straight ahead at the jury, I told my story. I focused totally on what I had to do. I made myself forget about who was in court or what anyone was thinking about me. I concentrated on what positive medical evidence we had. K had been described as 'well cared for' when admitted to hospital. Of normal weight and development. I was given my opportunity to tell the court that I'd been told, at first, that K had a neuroblastoma, a childhood cancer, and how this had terrified me. Yes, doctors had believed the injury was 'non-accidental', but a CT scan disclosed no damage to the skeletal frame. The medical report was of a 'lovely, well looked after child'. I told my story as clearly as I could.

Once I'd finished my testimony we had our opportunity to call our defence witnesses. We had only one – Father Brian McCanny. Since his only knowledge of the events surrounding the hospital admission was through me, he was appearing as a character witness. Based on his visits to my home.

I had been dreading Liam McCollum's cross-examination. We knew he would concentrate on the points that could be seen as weaknesses in my evidence. He pointed out that there was no mention of the baby making an 'abnormal cry' in my first police interview.

But I'd mentioned it in my second interview in March 2003.

'The reason you're remembering it now is because it's the only thing that will exonerate you,' he suggested.

'No,' I insisted. 'I want an answer to whatever happened to my baby. I don't know what happened to my baby. I'll take a lie detector test if you want me to and I think it should be done, because my baby nearly died and I don't know why.'

This was the first time I broke down in tears. I was allowed a short break. Carmel was at my side at once. I knew she was living every moment in the dock with me. She was my friend and my champion, not just my solicitor. She hugged me and told me I was doing well, and to keep it up.

Back in the dock, Mr McCollum made the case that I was the only person who could have hurt K.

'The truth is that you can provide no explanation whatever for the condition your baby was in when it was brought to hospital?'

'I thought it was colic,' I told him. How pathetic it sounded. But it was the truth.

The Prosecution made much of my circumstances at the time. Mr McCollum pointed out the facts in such a way as to evoke sympathy for me but it could also, I felt, have given a picture of a woman pushed to the limits of her capacity to cope. He reminded the jury that the late stages of my pregnancy had been marred by domestic rows. This had culminated in X leaving the home shortly before K was born. I had gone through childbirth without support from the father who had shown no signs of wanting to be involved in the child's upbringing. I also had a lively toddler, J, to care for. I must have been exhausted. I was dependent on benefits, and X had left me with debts to pay off. My parents, who might have been a source of support, were far away. I must have been depressed, he argued.

I could only assure the court that this was far from the case. It had been a relief when X walked out. The rows were over. The home was much happier and more stable with just me and the children. I'd been awarded a grant and was doing up the house – something I enjoyed. I was happy with my life in Derry and was taking steps to improve our circumstances. The court was told I had enrolled J and myself in the parenting programme Sure Start, which offers parents courses with free childcare and also brings together pre-school children for constructive play and early learning activities. The Prosecution tried to imply this meant I wasn't coping with J. K may have been a healthy baby but the Prosecution pointed out that although K was healthy, the baby had been bottle-fed. All my older children had been breastfed. Why? The Prosecution suggested that this implied a lack of bonding, even a lack of dedication.

The truth was, K simply didn't latch on to breast-feeding and was thriving on formula milk. It also made practical sense for me, with two tiny children to look after, single-handed.

Then, back to the day K was taken to hospital.

Mr McCollum reminded me I had had very little sleep the night before. Surely, he put it to me, I had simply 'lost my temper' and 'lashed out' at a crying baby?

'No,' I replied firmly.

'So who did it?'

'I don't know.'

Finally, had I harmed my baby?

'No.'

Exhausted, mentally, physically and emotionally, I left the stand and went back to the dock. The jury were ushered out for the day. The judge granted me my usual bail. I stepped out of the dock and almost collapsed into Carmel's arms.

Carmel had noticed that the reporters had seized on my offer to take a lie detector test. Sure enough, 'Mother offers to take lie test' was the *Belfast Telegraph*'s headline the next day. It was to prove more significant than I could have imagined.

THE SUMMING-UP

By Thursday I knew I'd done all I could. Carmel had told me that both sides would now sum up the evidence to keep it fresh in the minds of the jury members. The judge would add her direction to them. Then it was in their hands.

Junior counsel Russell Connell did the summing-up for the Prosecution. He told the court the Defence had 'put all its eggs in one basket' by suggesting that Peter could be responsible for injuring K. None of us thought that was how we'd set out our case. I had never blamed anyone – this fact had been confirmed in court. I had said I had no explanation for the injury and that I hadn't caused it. Not the same thing at all. But Mr Connell's remarks helped to set Janice and Peter's family against us as much as X's.

'The evidence about this man has changed between November 2002 and March 2003,' he said. 'We say, based on the evidence, that this injury was caused by the defendant. She had about two hours' sleep and the baby was unsettled all day.'

Ken McMahon made the opposite point in his summing-up for the Defence.

'The Prosecution are asking you [the jury] why would he do anything to the child? But why would SHE [me] do anything? We say there are other possibilities [he was referring to the neuroblastoma diagnosis here] and the Prosecution has not proved the case beyond reasonable doubt.' That was what I'd felt in my heart all along – the reason we couldn't work out who had harmed K was because K hadn't been harmed. There had to be another explanation.

Ken reminded the jury that the Prosecution had put forward a total of eight medical witnesses. Six of them had given their evidence in person; the other two had submitted written statements which had been accepted. Yet of these eight professional people only one had testified definitively that the injury was non-accidental and caused by some considerable degree of blunt force in a direct blow to the left kidney.

One in eight. I'd been told juries set a lot of store by simple clear statistics. Surely this was beneficial for us?

Then it was the turn of the judge to direct the jury. I knew how crucial this could be as the judge would effectively be reminding the jury of what she saw as the most relevant points in reaching a verdict.

Judge Philpott reminded the jury to consider that I was 'of good character'. At thirty-five, I had no convictions of any sort, and as such, I was more likely to be telling the truth. Yet she felt it was her duty to remind them that my four eldest children were not living with me. I shuddered when I heard this. Was this to be another moral judgement? More positively, the judge also reiterated that I had consistently denied harming K. Apart from omitting to mention the abnormal cry in the first police interview, my testimony had not wavered. Then she gave the jury the prescribed direction that to convict me on the more serious charge they must be convinced beyond reasonable doubt that I had intended to harm my baby. There was also the lesser charge, of causing grievous bodily harm without intent, to consider.

The jury retired to their room to consider their verdict. The court was cleared. Carmel, Michael, Ken and I sat in a huddle downstairs, nursing paper cups of coffee. I clutched my Saint Teresa prayer card to my chest. I was beyond fear. None of them needed to remind me that this was probably my last chance to be believed. By tomorrow I could be in the back of a prison van, starting a long sentence. Social workers could be telling J and K that Mummy Louise had done a bad thing and they were going to stay with their new family. All I could say was that I had done what I intended. I had told the truth. Would it be enough?

We made small talk, wondering how long it would be, whether anyone wanted another coffee. Mostly we sat in silence. Carmel had warned me that juries are notoriously unpredictable. She said she'd been watching them but they were impossible to gauge. She did think that they'd been attentive. A few of them had been taking notes. On our side, we had the truth, and my good character. But not one shred of medical evidence. No other suspect. I thanked my legal team once again. I cannot imagine any other three people could have cared more about the verdict. They really did want me to win.

There was nothing more we could do. It was out of our hands. I resigned myself to a long and agonising wait.

Leabharlanna Poibli Chathair Bhaile Átha Cliath
Dublin City Public Libraries

The Verdict

The call came just an hour and a half later. It took us all
by surprise. Carmel had explained to me earlier that a
quick verdict usually meant a unanimous one. We hurried up the stairs into court to wait for the jury to be
brought from their room. I remember there were five or
six reporters who were responsible for covering all the
local and national papers and radio and television
stations; they, too, were hurrying back upstairs, mutter-
ing among themselves and making predictions.

As the jury filed in they didn't make eye contact with
me or with Carmel. One woman had tears in her eyes.
Carmel told me later her heart sank. She thought this
woman had believed I was innocent and was upset because I was about to be sent down. I could scarcely
breathe. The tension was unbearable.

The courtroom fell silent as the clerk formally asked
the foreperson if the jury had reached a verdict upon
which they were all agreed.

'Yes.'

So it was unanimous. Carmel had been right.

'On the first count of causing grievous bodily harm with intent, do you find the defendant, Louise Jane Mason, guilty or not guilty?'

I thought my heart would stop.

'Not guilty.'

The next moments are a blur. I remember crying out 'Thank God!' and looking upwards, my prayer card clasped tight, and thanking Saint Teresa. I couldn't look round but I heard someone gasp, 'Yes'. Another woman called out, 'What about that wean?', or something like that. Carmel told me it was one of X's family and that several of them got up and walked out. One or two reporters hurried out, clutching their mobile phones, off to ring their newsrooms.

The hubbub gradually subsided.

The clerk asked the foreperson if they had reached a unanimous verdict on the second charge, of causing grievous bodily harm.

They had not.

Judge Philpott sent them out again, saying she would prefer a unanimous decision.

She called them back an hour later, at around six o'clock, and told them she would accept a majority verdict of eleven–one or ten–two. They hadn't reached that, either. She sent them home for the night with strict instruction not to discuss the case with anyone.

I couldn't let myself feel hopeful. Not yet. I had been

vindicated of intentionally harming K, but when it came to the lesser charge, the jury was divided. I knew that if they couldn't reach a majority verdict, I might have to face a retrial. That could take months to come to court.

On the way out of the building, a couple of reporters asked about arranging interviews for the next day, once the verdict was returned. That meant they thought I would be acquitted. Carmel gently shooed them away for the meantime.

We spent the night in limbo. I found it hard to suppress the little glimmer of hope inside. Carmel told me afterwards that she had felt the same way. But neither of us wanted to tempt fate.

'FREE TO GO'

As we walked into court the next day, Friday, to wait for the second verdict, I sensed a different atmosphere. The *Belfast Telegraph* had got the story in time for their morning edition: 'Woman is Cleared of Assaulting her Baby', read the headline. The first verdict had been reported on the radio news.

Carmel was not her usual calm self, but for a very different reason. She had divided loyalties that morning – her eldest child was sitting the Eleven Plus exam and she wanted to be there when her daughter came out. But she didn't want to leave me in court. In the end, she compromised. One of the reporters also had a daughter sitting the exam and the two of them paid a flying visit to the school playground, quickly established that their children were happy with their performance, and sped back to Court Four – just in time to catch the verdict.

It was just after half past eleven. The jury had been out for slightly over an hour.

Again, the clerk asked the foreperson if they had reached a verdict upon which they were all agreed.

'No.'

Had they reached a verdict on which ten or more of them were agreed?

'Yes.'

I'm told at least one woman juror looked across at me, but I was looking straight ahead. My mind was blank.

'And what is that verdict?

'Not guilty.'

This time there was no suppressing the volume as I cried 'Thank God!' and raised my eyes to heaven. I turned to the jury, crying 'Thank you, thank you!' I pressed my hands against the Perspex screen around the dock, tears streaming down my cheeks. I registered the words 'You are free to go.'

I walked over to where the female police officers were standing. I said to one officer, 'I hope you can find out who did this.' Her reply was: 'Get away from me, before I arrest you.' To say they were not at all happy about the verdict would be an understatement.

I saw Carmel coming towards me and we hugged each

other. She couldn't contain her joy. We knew the odds had been stacked against me. We had no medical evidence to support us. We couldn't explain why K had been so ill. But the jury had believed me. I can never thank those women and men enough. The truth was out. Our prayers had been answered. At long last.

Sally and her friend joined us, beaming. They had been great, all the way through. She was getting John on the phone to tell him the verdict. When I rang him outside the building, I could hear the delight in his voice. He had always believed in me.

Outside, once we were clear of the court building, reporters surrounded me for my comments. I had no statement prepared but I was happy to speak to them.

It's been a very long two years, but I've had the back up of a good legal team. I really hope the children are back with me and I want answers about what happened to K.

I kept praying. People believed in me, so I kept strong. When my baby was taken into hospital I prayed to Saint Teresa. I have to keep strong in my faith and God's good. I was praying for justice to be done, and justice has been done, but my first thought in the court was to get my babies back and that my youngest baby will now grow up knowing that I was not guilty. I have had no real hope for the last two years. Yesterday was my first real little bit of hope. Now there's a bit more. The sun is shining today.

It wasn't, it was a chill November sky, but it was shining in my heart. I finished with:

> I can cope, but my children have suffered the most over the past two awful years. I can't wait to see them again. I last saw them two weeks ago. Whatever it takes in court to get them back, I'll do it.

The headlines appeared: 'Cleared Mother Vows to Fight for Kids'; 'I'll fight to get them back'; 'I want my baby back'; 'Cleared Mum's daily prayer vigil'. I noticed that one of the papers that had carried the allegation that I'd battered my baby on the front page had tucked away the news of my acquittal on page six. It didn't really matter. That part of my struggle to clear my name was over. I knew I faced a long fight to get my children back. But at least they would grow up knowing that their mother had not harmed baby K.

My Fight for the Children Begins

There was no fairy-tale ending, however. Far from it. I suspect that many of the reporters and well-wishers who had surrounded me leaving the court expected J and K would now be back with me for good. Definitely by Christmas.

Half an hour after we'd walked out of the court, I was on the phone to my children in England. I promised them that we'd talk everything through when I was back in Northampton around Christmas. These things are difficult to explain and it would be much easier to do it face to face than on a mobile phone call. I also rang my parents and my sister. I particularly wanted to talk to Dad. He hadn't been keeping well and had been diagnosed with cancer. It wasn't thought to be life-threatening, but any cancer, however treatable, is serious. He and Mum were pleased for me, of course, but I don't think they'd realised how crucial the trial had been, or what I'd been going through for the past fortnight. Mum's attitude was the same as ever: if I'd done nothing wrong, then I had nothing to worry about. Mum and Deborah hadn't made it over to support me during the trial but I told myself not to feel disappointed or let down. My family's way has always been to let me get on with things by myself. I was trying to build bridges with Mum and we were back to talking on the phone for a few minutes each week.

When I was over at Christmas I also wanted to make my parents understand that the crime I'd been accused of was so serious that I could have spent the next ten years in jail. That J and K would have been adopted. I don't think any of my family really believed that this could happen. I couldn't tell them much about having to go back to the Family Court, or I'd have been in contempt of court, but I wanted to be able to explain why the children hadn't been handed straight back to me as soon as I was acquitted.

I was still desperate to know exactly what had happened to K in the hours before K was admitted to hospital. Maybe that first doctor had been right, and it had been an infant cancer, though how could K be so well now. K's health was still being monitored, but the symptoms hadn't come back. I had started to think that perhaps someone had dropped K, or accidentally hurt the baby, and then, once they heard the words 'non-accidental injury', they were too frightened to say anything.

Just over a fortnight after our victory in the Crown Court, we were back in the Family Division in Belfast's High Court. Even though I had been found not guilty of harming K, on 7 December 2004 the Foyle Trust proceeded with the application to have J and K freed for adoption. In its view, I was still an unfit mother. Carmel had warned me the Trust would change tack, and it did. Since I'd been acquitted at my trial, we knew it would be difficult for the Trust to claim it thought I was guilty of harming K. Its case for having J and K adopted now rested on it proving that I was an unfit mother.

Carmel made it clear to the court that we were resisting any moves to have the children adopted. She filed an affidavit to the effect that I did not accept the original care order ruling, and maintained my innocence regarding the Trust's claim and the court's finding that I had harmed K.

The court immediately ruled that my visits with J and K were to be increased, gradually, over a period of time. They would increase straightaway to one and a half hours each week, instead of each month. But the court also ruled that the visits would still have to take place in Shantallow Health Centre and a social worker would supervise me throughout.

What kept me going throughout the Christmas period was the knowledge that things could only improve now. My relationship with John was good and I was a regular visitor to his family's home. Everyone made me welcome, with invitations to visit them, to try to compensate for

J and K spending Christmas with their foster family. As in previous years, I'd taken them their presents a few days before Christmas, on the day the community centre closed for the holidays. J was buzzing with excitement and I had to hold back the tears; I would have given anything to see that little face on Christmas Eve, or to tuck my two-year-old up and read *The Night Before Christmas*. Little rituals are a very intimate part of every family's life. But these were denied to us.

I went to Northampton shortly after Christmas to see my other four children. I was able to stay with my parents for a few days. Their health had deteriorated. Dad had been having treatment for his cancer and Mum was still suffering from bouts of depression. We all discussed the court case and I told them the whole story, for the first time. I think the seriousness of the situation was finally becoming clear to them.

Over the past two years, I'd been going to Northampton as often as I could. I couldn't afford to go as much as I would have liked. During these flying visits, the children often had their own routines and I tried to slot into everyday life as much as possible, and enjoy it. Now I was able to take time to sit with Jaz, Nina and Ayshea and go through all the details; there were no more court restrictions on me discussing my trial with them. The children immediately and understandably asked when I was returning to Northampton. They really wanted me to come back. Now the trial was over, surely there was nothing to stop me?

Once again, I was caught in the heart of a dilemma. Nina had told me she wasn't getting on well with her father; she found him too controlling and dictatorial, and they fought a lot. Ayshea had become very spirited, like her sister, so she wasn't happy living with Sol and his wife, either. Jaz seemed content but, at nearly sixteen, he was concentrating on his studies and hoping to go to college. He seemed to avoid the rows. Jake was still too young, at seven, to understand properly what was going on. He was very settled and happy with Trevor but he told me he would have loved me to live near them and to 'see me lots'.

Jaz, Nina and Ayshea assured me that if I moved back to England, they would all come to live with me and keep in touch with their father. I was really torn. I knew Mum would never be able to have my teenagers living with her again, because of her health. The three older ones called round to her on a regular basis, but they couldn't move back in to live with her and Dad. They weren't free to move to Ireland and, anyway, they didn't want to – it would have been taking them away from all their friends, their school and my parents. And, one way or the other, Sol was still part of their equation.

I talked to Carmel and we sounded out the Trust to see what would happen to J and K if I wanted to move back to England. I was told there was no chance whatsoever of them being fostered in Northampton. If I moved back there to live, I would find it impossible to keep up weekly access visits – I wouldn't be able to afford the travel costs

– and most definitely wouldn't be able to cope if the visits increased to twice and three times a week, as was planned. So, if I left Derry, I'd be abandoning J and K and the Trust would then have strong grounds for putting them up for adoption.

I spent many sleepless nights, thinking it through, but in the end decided I had to stay in Derry. My older children were well looked after and I went to Northampton as often as I could. Once they were adults, they could live where they wanted. Also, they had their fathers and their maternal grandparents near them. They had no one in Ireland, except me, J and K. And if I left Derry, J and K would have no one. I had to stay in Ireland.

Over the holiday, Carmel had been keeping a secret from me – for the best possible reason. She didn't want to raise false hope; she'd been at my side through too many disappointments already. But, just days after I'd been acquitted in the Crown Court, she'd received the vital phone call that would introduce her to the man we came to regard as our guardian angel, and set in motion the chain of events that is bringing K home for good.

Late one afternoon, at the start of December, Carmel's secretary told her a gentleman was on the line, someone who had called earlier and left a message and who was insisting he must be put through to her. Urgently. It was almost time for the office to close, and Carmel was, as ever, inundated with work. His name didn't mean anything to her, but she agreed to take the call from the man we have called Dr D. He identified himself as a consultant radiologist at Altnagelvin Hospital and provided details of his qualifications and experience. He told Carmel that he'd been leafing through a copy of the *Belfast Telegraph* when a headline on a court report caught his eye: 'Mother offers to take lie test'. As he read on, Dr D realised that the details struck a chord with him. The report didn't mention my name, or K's, but he thought it must be a case he had been involved in some years earlier. He described my case. Could Carmel confirm this was the same woman? Indeed she could.

Dr D was shocked. He was one of the first people to examine K, but no one had ever contacted him about the case. No one had told him the child had been taken into care or that the mother had been prosecuted for allegedly harming the baby. No one had asked for his medical reports or his X-rays. Dr D couldn't understand why he had been ignored when so many other medical witnesses were interviewed at length. He would have been happy to go to court and testify that K had a neuroblastoma, a child cancer that often does go into remission, quickly and permanently.

It posed a number of questions. Why had the detectives investigating the case not looked for him? It would have seemed sensible to interview the first doctor who examined K when K was brought into Altnagelvin Hospital. If K had been harmed, he would have been the first one to see the physical evidence. Dr D told us he had made medical case notes on K, but that neither the police nor the Prosecution had asked him for access to them. Nor had they asked to see K's X-rays. Even though it was clear that the Prosecution had a number of strong medical witnesses, he would have expected to be contacted. But he had never heard another word about K's case after the child was taken to the Royal. He hadn't even been told K's illness was being treated as non-accidental.

Dr D was horrified to discover my children were still in care. Why? he demanded. The doctor recalled there had been a 'wide divergence of opinion' in the case. He, personally, had been confident the baby had suffered a neuroblastoma and there was no suspicion of non-accidental injury. He was mystified as to how my case had ever gone to court.

Carmel was stunned. She hadn't known he existed. I have only a hazy memory of the staff who were on duty that night. I couldn't remember their names or their faces. Carmel immediately realised this was the evidence that could clear my name for good. But she also knew how difficult it could be for Dr D to come forward publicly. It would mean breaking ranks with his colleagues. It could jeopardise his job with the same Trust that had taken the children into care. Cautiously, she asked him if he was prepared to make a sworn affidavit about what he'd just told her. Dr D confirmed that he was.

On 15 February 2005, he did just that. And I was let in on the wonderful news that this good and brave man was prepared to stand up and be counted, to ask the Prosecution team why he had not been told what was happening, and why they had not looked for his evidence. I was delighted to be able to meet him in person to thank him. I found him a real gentleman. He did what he knew was right. As a result of his concerns, and following Carmel's request, the application to free J and K for adoption was adjourned to allow my legal team to make further inquiries.

Dr D advised us to get a report from an independent consultant paediatric radiologist. He further advised that any report obtained should be commented upon by an independent consultant paediatrician with a particular interest in the subject and occurrence of non-accidental injury. Dr D advised that the independent consultant paediatric radiologist and the independent consultant paediatrician should be requested to comment with specific regard to how the findings of the medical witnesses quoted in the courts correlated with K's medical history when admitted to hospital, the examination findings and laboratory results.

A consultant paediatric radiologist was instructed. He provided a report, dated 19 May 2005, and then two further notes, dated 29 May 2005 and 20 June 2005. He did not rule out the possibility of K having suffered from a naturally occurring condition, as raised by Dr D.

A consultant paediatrician was then instructed and he provided a report, dated August 2005. This report recommended that either a paediatric nephrologist or a paediatric endocrinologist should be instructed to comment further and in more precise detail about whether, based on the evidence, K was more likely to have suffered from non-accidental injury than a naturally occurring condition.

The report of the nephrologist, dated 31 November 2005, was the one my legal team had been waiting for. The breakthrough at last. The nephrologist advised that 'in his opinion it seemed that a spontaneous haemorrhage, ie. a naturally occurring disease, provided the more comprehensive explanation of the findings' and he 'raised concern' that the appropriate investigations for neuroblastoma were not undertaken at the time of K's admission to hospital, either at Altnagelvin or at the Royal Belfast Hospital for Sick Children. A simple urine test would have confirmed that K was suffering from a neuroblastoma. A specific blood test should also have detected it.

To date, we have been unable to find out whether these tests were ever carried out; and, if they were, what became of the results.

Chloe

I was lucky to get to visit my older children almost every month in 2005. Staying at my parents' home again meant I only had to save up for the flights, and train or bus fare. In between, we talked on the phone and sent text messages to one another. Jaz, Nina and Ayshea were in their teens and were enjoying summer jobs and hectic social lives, and Jake was eight and thriving. By the autumn, I'd moved from my flat to a rented terrace house in the university area of the city. J, who was now four, had started P1 and was able to understand a little more about why we were living the way we were. I had missed another milestone – that first day at school – but I tried not to dwell on it. Surely I'd be there for the next one.

I had an extra reason for home-making. John and I had learned we were expecting a baby, due in February 2006. My friends were happy for us, my health was good, and 2006 seemed to offer all sorts of possibilities for a fresh start as a family.

I had reckoned without two things – malicious interference, and John's growing fears about fatherhood. The pregnancy wasn't planned and John made it clear he hadn't intended to have any more children. He already had a grown-up daughter who didn't live with him. His family got on well with me and supported me, especially Sally. But he began drifting away from me, and I discovered he was seeing another woman.

I was facing another Christmas alone. Sally insisted I should come to her for my dinner and I did so, appreciating the invitation. I woke up alone, on Christmas morning, walked to her house, stayed an hour or so and walked back to my own empty home. I had given J and K their presents a week before, and they were with their foster family, a couple of miles away. Jake was with Trevor, and Jaz, Nina and Ayshea were with Sol, and visiting my parents. It was another dark and lonely time. Then, on 27 December, I got a call to tell me that Mum had suffered a heart attack on Christmas Eve. I got the first available flight to England. She survived, but it was the beginning of more health troubles.

When I came back to Derry in January 2006, just a month before the baby was due, John turned up at my house to end the relationship for good. He said he'd been told that I'd had a one-night stand with X. Nothing could have been more ridiculous. The fact that I had once had a barring order against X and had no contact with him didn't convince John that this was malicious gossip. He also claimed that he'd been shown social services reports that described how I had 'abandoned' my older children. I'd been honest with him about this from the start, explaining how it all had come about. I suspected that social services didn't approve of me having another baby and wanted to shake John's confidence in my ability to be a good mother. They succeeded.

Then John said he didn't know that the baby was his and demanded that I take a DNA test when it was born. (There was no need to, I'd been faithful to him, but I took the test anyway. John is Chloe's father. He has never visited her or supported her financially.) John also told his mother and other family members that they must decide where their loyalty lay – with him and his new girlfriend, or with me. They never fell out with me, but they didn't get in touch and drifted away.

I felt betrayed again. And once more I felt that I was being punished for something I hadn't done. John had been my boyfriend for eighteen months, although we hadn't lived together. I had never thought it would end like this; that I would raise another little one without its father. I was furiously angry with the people who, I am convinced, did their utmost to destroy our relationship. I was only sorry it had not been strong enough to stand the test.

Around the same time, there was further progress on the legal front. A paediatric oncologist, who had been instructed to comment further and in more precise detail on the paediatric radiologist's report on K, delivered his findings on 31 January 2006. He said that he considered that a neuroblastoma was the likely explanation of K's illness.

Finally, I seemed to have an answer. I thought back to the long days and nights when I had tortured myself about what had happened to baby K. Now I knew. No one had harmed K. There had been no injury, accidental or non-accidental. The infant had been suffering from a cancer, a neuroblastoma, which, mercifully, had gone into remission and disappeared, as, I was told, it often does. Relief outweighed the anger that one simple urine test could have established this, within hours, once and for all. How much needless grief, how much anguish for my children and for me could have been avoided. How much sooner my young family would have been reunited. I was also angry that this meant K had not been given the proper treatment for the neuroblastoma. It was only fortunate that it had disappeared naturally.

My legal team then informed the Family Division that we were going to make an application to the Court of Appeal to reverse the care order ruling. While this was pending, we applied to have adjourned generally the Foyle Trust's application to free J and K for adoption. It seemed to be only a matter of time now before they were back with me. And the new baby.

Chloe was born at twenty past two on the morning of 6 February 2006. Adele and Frankie had insisted I stay with them over the weekend that the baby was due. Adele brought me to the labour ward at Altnagelvin and, as she had promised, she stayed with me throughout. For me, the hospital was associated with grief and loss. The whole nightmare had begun with K's emergency admission there. It was here that the social services had taken K from me to hand over to foster parents. But the medical staff were great and my new baby arrived safe and well. I was determined to breastfeed, if I could.

I was lying back, resting, with Chloe in the cot beside my bed, tired but content. Everything had gone well. Chloe was a beautiful baby. At around half past four in the morning, while I was still in the labour ward, a midwife came over to my bed and explained to me that she would have to take Chloe to the neonatal unit. Social services had been in touch with the hospital and advised them that I should not be allowed to be on my own with my baby. I was distraught. The midwife told me that she was very sorry but she was obliged to remove the baby.

Adele tried to comfort me but soon after staff came to take me to the postnatal ward and Adele was not allowed to come with me. In shock and exhausted, I decided the only thing I could do was phone Carmel. I waited until it was almost nine o'clock and then I rang her on my mobile.

Carmel knew my baby was due and she told me later that for one confused moment she wondered if the call was an excited Louise, bearing good news. It wasn't. I was hysterical, begging her to get over to the maternity unit as quickly as possible.

Carmel made it to Altnagelvin in record time. She says

the scene that greeted her was surreal. She was directed to the neonatal unit, despite her protests that my baby must have been full term. She was led into the ward full of tiny scraps of premature infants, lying in incubators, each connected to a maze of wires and monitors. Medical staff monitored their every heartbeat, their every little breath, and tired and anxious parents kept a constant vigil. And there, in the midst of these infants, who were struggling to survive, was baby Chloe Mason, bouncing with health, shouting lustily for the mother she'd been taken from. It was too cruel, Carmel says. She could not believe anyone in authority could do this. Besides what it was doing to me, it was so insensitive to the feelings of everyone in that ward.

Carmel demanded to know what was going on. She discovered that I was in the postnatal ward, on the floor above, and that I had opted to breastfeed my baby. So why had my baby and I been separated? Who had authorised it? Carmel, who has three children herself, is not fazed by crying babies and is an imposing and persistent woman when the occasion demands it. The nursing sister told her that the Trust had stipulated that I was not to be left alone with the baby after it was born. A premeditated move by the Trust, then. We knew nothing about it. We had no warning. Carmel told the nursing staff they had no legal authority to do this and insisted on speaking to the person responsible.

The medical staff were in a quandary. They tried to contact the duty social worker but he could not be reached. The baby was patently the picture of health. My antenatal reports showed no cause for concern. It had been a textbook pregnancy. Emergency consultations and negotiations began. But it was Chloe who took action. She demanded to be fed.

The staff suggested I should be brought down to feed her. I was to sit in the middle of ward, with no screens or privacy, and in full view of the mothers whose babies could only feed through a network of tubes. It would have been such a painful contrast. Carmel retorted that no one would treat an animal who'd just given birth this way, never mind a woman. She fought our case all morning, not from a courtroom bench nor a judge's chambers, but from the middle of a neonatal unit, until little Chloe was safely back in the cot beside my bed.

The next day two social workers came to meet with me and the head midwife of the postnatal unit. The social workers informed me that I was not allowed to leave the hospital with Chloe and if I attempted to do so the Trust would be within its rights to contact the police and have me arrested. I was devastated but Carmel made it clear to me that there was no way we could fight this. The head midwife did what she could for me, and agreed to let me and Chloe stay in the postnatal unit for almost two weeks, much longer than can reasonably be expected. The staff could not have been more helpful or kind to us while we were there.

But there was no escaping the inevitable. The Trust

had applied for, and got, an interim care order for my baby. Chloe would not be going home with me. Chloe would be fostered. To me, there was not, and cannot, be any justification for this action. The reason given was that the care order over J and K was still extant. But how can a Health Trust consider it better to foster the baby of a mother who has been acquitted in a Criminal Court of assaulting another child? A child who, medical evidence had now shown, was never assaulted in the first place, but had been suffering a form of cancer? They had absolutely no grounds for this.

By the time the interim care order was enforced, Chloe and I had established a pattern of breastfeeding, so I was allowed to have my baby brought to my home for six hours every day, from 2 to 8 p.m. I kept a feeding diary, which went to and from the foster family and was filled in meticulously. The feeding visits were supervised by members of the family support team; they were mature women who were very supportive to me. They worked two-hour shifts, so I got to know and like most of them. They soon realised I was a calm and competent mother who kept a clean and tidy house and enjoyed her baby very much. Every smile, every gurgle, every movement, every cuddle was all the more poignant because I had been deprived of these simple joys with K. Every health report showed that Chloe was thriving, well cared for and content. Like her mum, in fact, when she was with her. One of the support workers became a good friend and remains so.

I brought Chloe to meet J and K when she was just a couple of weeks old. This was a sign that things were becoming more flexible, although we were still tied to Shantallow Health Centre. The family support team had given me a list of questions the children were likely to ask about us, as a family, and the answers I should give them. It didn't cover everything, but it helped. J and K doted on their baby half-sister from the start and still hold her and cuddle her at every opportunity, telling her they love her. It's wonderful to watch them together.

On 1 March 2006, the Court of Appeal considered our application on J and K and duly quashed the previous Family Court ruling of April 2004. The care order application regarding J and K was referred back to the Family Division for a rehearing. This was scheduled to begin on 5 June.

At the end of March, Chloe was christened, at what was then my home parish, St Eugene's Cathedral. Sally had agreed to be godmother. She still spoke to me and I respected the dilemma John had put her in – choosing between him and his new girlfriend, and me. Two days before the christening, however, Sally stopped answering my calls. At the last minute, when it was clear she wasn't going to turn up, Carmel stepped into the breach. I couldn't wish for a better godmother for Chloe.

That June, we entered the Family Court with some degree of confidence. The Trust opened the case by listing all the aspects of the proposed care order for J and K that had been put forward at the first hearing. The

court allowed some time for discussions and consultations with the medical witnesses. Then the Trust said
the words we had been hoping for – that it did not intend
to call any evidence in respect of the allegation of non-
accidental injury to K. The doctors' reports were referred
to the court, which, as a formality, ruled that, on the
balance of probability, the allegation of non-accidental
injury could no longer form part of the case for imposing
a care order on J and K. It had been dismissed as a cause
of K's illness.

On the advice of my legal team, I agreed to go along
with the proposed care plans for the children. To oppose
them would have brought me into direct confrontation
with the Trust, and that would not have been in the
children's best interests. This meant that, provided I continued to cooperate with the family support workers and
involve myself in any therapy or counselling specified for
me, all three children would be back home 'at varying
times to be determined by their needs'. J and K would
also be given specialist counselling to help them understand what had happened.

Chloe was returned to me on a permanent basis in
July, just weeks after the court ruling. Both J and K
enjoyed spending as much time as possible with the
baby. The Trust's information guidelines about how to
answer their questions was increasingly put to the test.
And as time goes on I know my children's enquiries will
become more searching and the answers will have to be
more detailed. I've kept a memory box for the children,

with all my newspaper cuttings, and personal items like Chloe's feeding diary. When they are older, they can read the evidence for themselves. Then they will know that I never let them down, and never abandoned them.

Going to and from Northampton was more difficult with a small baby, but we made it in the summer and Chloe was introduced to my other children, who were also very taken with this blonde bundle. My parents love her, of course, and one of my regrets is that J, K and Chloe will not get to know their paternal grandparents, and aunts and uncles who live so near to them in Derry. But that is their fathers' decision, not mine, and we Masons have enough love for them all.

J spent more and more time at home over the coming months. Now in P2, J was settling well into a routine and was happy to be spending a lot more time with me. I had applied for, and was allocated, a Housing Executive tenancy in the Ballymagroarty area of Derry, which suited all our needs – convenient for school, church and shops. I moved in during May 2006 and was given a grant to do it up.

By the summer, both J and K were with me three times a week. Jake came over, as planned, and the four children and I had some great times, playing in the open spaces around our new home, with scooters, roller skates, bikes and a trike. We got an aquarium and they took turns looking after the fish. They all had fun whatever they did – dressing up, making up games, or going shopping with me, all holding hands. I am so proud of them. They are such loving, caring children.

We had a welcome surprise in the autumn – Nina came to live with us. She was now sixteen and at loggerheads with her father. She felt the need to get away for a while, to think things out. She was great company and a real help, but I could tell she was very undecided about her future. She didn't make many friends in Derry and missed Northampton. When Chloe and I went over at Christmas, Nina came too, and stayed. But her time in Derry definitely strengthened the bond between us and we are in contact a lot more often. Nina has now moved out of her father's home and into a flat with her boyfriend, and has a full-time job.

The pieces of my family jigsaw were falling into place; even if it bemused my new neighbours a little. (How many children *did* I have?) For the first time in years, I began to make positive plans for the future that extended beyond the immediate goal of reuniting my family under my own roof. While I was determined to enjoy every minute of watching J, K and Chloe grow up, I vowed never to lose sight of how easily that might have been lost forever. And I promised myself that I would do everything within my power to win the right to go public about my case; to reach out to support other mothers who may be facing, or have faced, a similar nightmare. Finally, I pledged that I would try to raise funds to set up a warm, friendly centre where parents and children separated by the Family Courts could meet in an atmosphere as close as possible to a home environment. I knew from experience what a difference that would make to those precious hours.

J Comes Home
for Good

December 2007 was a wonderful month. Six-year-old J came home, for good. J had no problems adjusting and had always thought of me as the 'real Mummy'. Now a happy, healthy P3 pupil, J, like Chloe, is very loving and close to me.

It had been stressful organising everything by the clock to fit in with the times when J and K were coming and going between their foster home and me. Now, at last, J and I could begin to relax into things. We could start making Christmas decorations, knowing that if the paint wasn't dry at bedtime, we could finish them the next day. One window on the Advent calendar was opened cere-monially every morning; they didn't have to be opened two or three at a time in two separate homes. I didn't have to remember which clothes were in which house. We went shopping together for new outfits – there was plenty of time to try them on, rather than me having to buy things I hoped would fit. I bought all J's favourite foods – J advised me about K's.

I'd already had their rooms redecorated and the house gleamed from top to bottom. Everything we did together was relaxed and fun. J could tell classmates, with confidence, that Mummy would be at the nativity play and at the carol concert (and be the proudest Mummy there). I'd waited so long to be involved in every part of J's life that I was determined not to miss a single moment of it.

We hoped very much that K would be with us over Christmas. I knew how disappointed we would be if it didn't work out. I didn't have it confirmed until a few days before, but K was with us throughout the day, to celebrate our first ever family Christmas together. It was the day I had longed for. The four of us, sitting round the tree at a ridiculously early hour, ripping the wrapping paper off Santa's gifts and eating chocolate in our pyjamas. Later, a huge meal with party hats and crackers, then outdoors to play with the scooter and roller skates. More games, Disney classics on television, telephone calls to Northampton, where I didn't need to describe what we were doing – the happiness in my voice, the background chorus of animated chatter and the squeals of laughter said it all. Exhausted at the end of the day, as my three sleepy children snuggled up to me, and I surveyed the adventure playground that had once been my orderly living room, I was blissfully happy.

My priorities now were to clear my name in public

and, most importantly, to have K, who's now almost six, back with us for good. J had absolutely no problems adapting to life with me and Chloe, even though J and I hadn't lived together in the same house for five years. Perhaps this is partly because J was with me for the first two years and has never thought of me as anything but Mummy. Also, at seven, coming eight, J can understand a lot more about what happened to us.

I am really looking forward to the day when we are all under one roof, at last, but I'm trying to be realistic about how long it may take. K was just four weeks old when we were separated. We missed out on the chance to bond. I find it very hard watching K playing with the others, knowing how much I love them all and want them with me, but having to face the fact that K still finds it difficult to understand that I am the birth, or 'real' Mummy. For the first five years, K understood the foster parents to be Mummy and Daddy, and their home was home to K.

Both houses are full of love for K, but they aren't the same and can't be. I now welcome the chance to chat to K's foster mother when the child is dropped off and collected, but both of us know that the Trust advises against our forming a personal bond. I've never been to K's foster home, for example, and I've never met her foster father. Our circumstances are very different. With J back at home with me, K's the only young child in the foster home and has quickly become used to one-to-one adult attention. In our home, I have to share my time and attention among J, K and Chloe. Similarly, K has recently been treated to luxuries that I can't afford; two holidays abroad and trips to the foster family's holiday home in Ireland where they spend part of the summer, and weekends throughout the year. While K is dividing time between the foster family and me, it's impossible to treat K in exactly the same way as J and Chloe. I try to explain that there are some things we do in different ways, and that neither way is right or wrong, but I can see it's confusing for K. I feel social services should arrange regular counselling sessions and some sort of family therapy to help us handle the move home in the best possible way for all of us. This had been suggested, but once I'd overturned the care order in the Family Division, I was left very much on my own. I feel the therapy we received wasn't intensive enough. I have been allocated a family support worker who comes to the house after school, three days a week, for an hour or so, to help J with homework in term time. This leaves me free to spend more time with K, or K and Chloe together. She's great, but a few more hours would be really helpful.

I was excited, and also apprehensive, the first time K was to sleep overnight with us. But K found the whole idea very difficult, missed the familiar surroundings of the foster home and asked to be taken back. I was disappointed and also worried that K would never want to stay overnight with us. The second attempt was a little more successful, but K was awake and out of bed several times in the night.

Gradually, we're all getting used to it. Just because

the law directs that a child who has been separated from its birth mother for most of its life is to be returned to her, doesn't mean that it can happen overnight. Judge Gillen was right when he acknowledged in his judgment that this would have to be done in a 'phased, planned way'. Relationships have to be strengthened, the past has to be explained, and everyone involved has to make adjustments.

Now the usual routine is that K comes for an evening visit, twice a week, and stays over on Friday nights. During the evening visits, I'm always conscious of the pressure of time; K's just getting nice and comfortable with us when it's time to go back to the foster home, and get bathed and settled down for bed. We have a better chance to do things together on Friday nights, but, again, after lunchtime each Saturday, we're all conscious that K is waiting to be collected.

In April 2008, K's foster family were on holiday abroad and we didn't see K for more than a fortnight. J and K are very close – after all, they were fostered together for five years – and miss each other terribly when they're apart. It's also difficult to explain why one of them can do things like miss school to go abroad, and the other can't. I love the feeling when all three children are together. Watching them hold hands walking to the shops brings a big smile to my face.

I wish K was back with me full time and, on down days, I worry it may never happen. I have to remind myself that K was living apart from me during the most important bonding period for mother and child. I'm trying to come to terms with the fact that the mother–child bond is not there as it should be with K, and I'm trying to do what's best for us all. But sometimes when I watch my children playing together, I am overwhelmed by sadness, realising that one of them does not really know me as more than a friendly, loving adult. It really hurts.

The social services have said they think things may work out naturally when K is eleven – the age at which they expect children to make their own way to and from school, establish their independence, and make their own decisions. It seems a long time away, to me, with many, many days of not living fully in one home or the other.

Relations with my older children are different, but very strong. They are young adults now. Jaz is nineteen this year, lives in a shared house with student friends and is at college studing computer technology. Nina, who is eighteen, has set up home with her partner and is working full-time. Ayshea, who's seventeen, wants to apply to an airline and train to become a cabin crew member as soon as she's old enough. Jake is a happy and secure eleven-year-old, living with Trevor in term-time and thrilled to be able to join us all in Derry in the holidays. We are also planning our first family trip to Northampton – J, K, Chloe and me. It'll be K's first visit.

I have come to accept that Mum, Dad, Stephen, Deborah and I are as close as we are ever likely to be; there's no point in trying to make things what they aren't.

But the rift with Mum has been healed to a large extent. My parents are getting older and my dream would be, one day, to buy a small flat in Northampton to have a base there for regular trips over. For now, Derry is home. Deborah and I stay in contact by phone, and I've been in touch with Stephen in Devon for the first time in years. I think we will stay in touch, too.

I'm determined to make the best possible life for us all. I've redecorated the house from top to bottom, and signed up for a parenting course. My friends from the prayer group will always be important to me, part of my circle of old and trusted friends; I owe a lot to Jean and Colum, Monsignor McCanny, and Adele and Frankie. I've become involved in another prayer group at Termonbacca. I first went there three years ago, when I was feeling low. It's specifically for people who have come through very tough, traumatic times in their lives, with their faith strengthened.

I've bought a computer and am learning to use it, much to the amusement of my eldest, Jaz. But it does make keeping in touch with Northampton much easier as the e-mails fly back and forth. I take J and K horse-riding. I'm having driving lessons for the first time. We live near some of Ireland's most beautiful coastline and beaches, so it'd be great to be able to take my family for days out. I feel I'm getting back my confidence.

There will be setbacks along the way, I know, but my mood, as I finish this book, is positive and determined – and hopeful. Writing has left me emotionally drained at times; it has brought me to tears; it has been a reminder of how far we have come, and with that has come a strong sense of self-worth, and pride that I never stopped fighting for my children. Jaz, Nina, Ayshea, Jake, J, K, and Chloe. I love every one of them, and am loved in return. That's what makes my whole, painful, extraordinary struggle worthwhile. I have lived through a mother's nightmare. Looking back, I can't believe I got through it. I'm trying to come to terms with the past and to look to the future. Most of all, I'm enjoying every precious minute with my children, now that we're finally back together, which is all I ever wanted.

Afterword

If my priority has always been to have my three youngest children back living with me, all the time, then a close second has been to clear my name in public. To do that, I needed to be free to tell my story. My legal team spent almost two years petitioning the Family Court for a relaxation of restrictions on publicity for my case. We never breached the ban on publicity, and the handful of journalists who had followed the case since the criminal proceedings had respected the court ruling, too. Two dates were scheduled to hear our application in 2007. Both were adjourned. The second hearing was called off just half an hour before it was due to start. This was frustrating, as we'd already made the journey to Belfast, hoping it would be for the last time.

Our final day in court eventually came on 20 February 2008. Carmel had told me to expect good news. The media were on standby and reporters had warned me I'd be the subject of widespread attention –

my ruling was going to make news, not just in Northern Ireland but across the UK. It would be a real precedent if the judge allowed the reporting restrictions to be relaxed my case.

I think people need to know what goes on in a Family Court. I couldn't forget how ignorant I had been of the way they work until I found myself appearing in one. Hearings in Family Courts are held in private and they can't be reported on, to protect the children whose lives are discussed, and that's only right and proper. But I wasn't aware that, at that time, a social work team could ask a judge to hear an application to have a child taken into care, for example, without the child's parents knowing anything about it. Or having a chance to be legally represented. Thankfully, the law has now changed so that what happened to me cannot be repeated. Imagine the horror of being at your seriously ill baby's bedside, in hospital, and finding out, not only that your elder child has been made the subject of an Emergency Care order, but that the order has already been enforced without you knowing anything about it. The first time a parent may know about it is when the ruling is enforced and social workers take the child away. That's what happened to me. I understand that, in some cases, such drastic and immediate intervention may be necessary. But not in mine. And because of the restrictions on publicity governing Family Court cases I was forbidden by law from contacting an empathic, authoritative figure to ask them to lobby my case. Had I done so, it would have been contempt of court and punishable by a fine or imprisonment.

I also think Family Courts give social workers too much power. They can decide that a parent isn't fit to look after a child, and get a court order to have that child taken into care, without producing any hard evidence. They are free to make an unfair moral judgement. Put simply, in my case my children were first taken into care because a doctor made a mistake, and the judge made his ruling based on faulty medical evidence. I believe they were then kept in care because social workers believed that a mother who had left her four older children in England, and whose seven children had four different fathers, was an unfit parent. When such a judgement is made about a parent, he or she can lose their children, even if they have no criminal convictions, no psychiatric illness, and no history of substance misuse. And I am living proof of how difficult it is to get them back.

It is my belief, shared by the lobby group Portia, that if I had been a middle-class, professional woman with a husband from a similar background, living in an affluent area, the social services would have been less likely to take this action against me. Conversely, if I had been uneducated, inarticulate, ground down by years of un-employment and poverty, or in poor physical or mental health, I would not have stood an iota of a chance in taking on the system, and J, K and Chloe would have been adopted.

Another reason for going public was to help other

mothers who were going through the same type of thing. Even if it was only to let them know that I knew, as well, what it was like to feel the whole world was against you. The memory of those first eight months after I was charged will stay with me forever. In darker times I had taken comfort from reading about other women who had won through against the legal system. Within a week of winning my Crown Court case, back in November 2004, I'd been told that my acquittal was mentioned on the website of the miscarriage of justice group, Portia. I looked up their site to find out more about the group.

The Portia Campaign evolved from a registered charity called the Portia Trust. This was set up by an international journalist, Ken Norman, after he had reported on a baby-snatching case in 1971; he thought the sentence imposed on the woman involved, who had suffered the loss of her own baby and was clearly very unwell, was too harsh. The Portia Trust was set up to support the cases of women, in particular, who had been wrongfully convicted or given unduly harsh sentences for crimes, or alleged crimes, usually involving children. Ken Norman died in October 2003 and since then the Portia Campaign has been maintained by a group of professionals from the legal, medical and media world who share his concern at what sometimes passes for justice in the UK. They take their philosophy from an eighteenth-century legislator, Sir William Blackstone, whose book *Commentary on the Laws of England* is still in use in courts today. He said it was 'better that ten guilty persons escape than one innocent suffer'. Most judges don't seem to accept his belief.

As I was browsing through the Portia site, one case stood out to me. It involved a mother of four from Wiltshire, called Angela Cannings. I recognised her name from an article I'd read in a magazine or newspaper and now I was able to find out what had happened to her.

Angela Cannings was put on trial after her eighteen-week-old son Matthew died suddenly in 1999. The family had already lost a son, Jason, eight years earlier, when he was seven weeks old. She was charged with smothering both her sons, convicted and sentenced to life.

Two things secured her release – the medical expert who had testified against her, Professor Sir Roy Meadow, had been discredited in the courts by the time her case came to appeal. And a team of journalists had helped her trace her family to Ireland and discovered a genetic link to sudden infant death syndrome (SIDS). Angela and Terry Cannings's first child, Gemma, had died of SIDS aged thirteen weeks, in 1989. One of Angela's Irish relatives had lost five children to SIDS.

When she walked free from the Appeal Court in 2003, Angela Cannings said it was the end of a four-year nightmare. She told reporters:

> After having previously lost our precious Gemma and Jason, we thought we had been through enough heartache. Then there was a police investigation, a trial

and a conviction. Finally today, justice has been done and my innocence has been proven.

There was so much here that I could identify with. Angela Cannings had been convicted on unreliable medical evidence. That had nearly happened to me. She paid great tribute to her legal team. I had done the same. She had been helped by the media to establish a genetic link to SIDS. A newspaper headline had brought Dr D to us. Some members of the media had highlighted my case in a responsible and unbiased way.

Another campaigner, Penny Mellor, had written about six women she knew personally who had social services take away their babies at birth, for no valid reason. That was exactly what happened with Chloe.

I began to read everything I could about cases like mine. Over the past four years, I've taken the time to collect and put in order all my newspaper cuttings. They'll be something for my children to look through in the future. I don't have many mementos from K's early childhood; very few photographs, little clothes or toys that have been cuddled to bits. This file will help to explain why.

Back to February 2008, and that crucial ruling by the judge, Mr Justice Gillen. He said he had decided to relax the normal prohibitions on publicity in a Family Court case, even though, he accepted, this could lead indirectly to the identification of the children. He went so far as to issue a news release to the media and to post the ruling on the Northern Ireland Courts website.

Summing up my case, Judge Gillen explained that he had dealt with a rehearing of a case where a care order had been imposed. He had found that I should have my children returned in a 'phased, planned way'. He said this was 'in the light of a change in the medical view'. The allegation of non-accidental injury, which had led to the children being taken away, was no longer part of the case against me.

The judge concluded that because the case was already known in the area where we live, because disclosure would 'assist the mother to address her sense of injustice', and because the workings of the family justice system in this case were matters of public interest, some publicity was appropriate. He said he had reached this conclusion after balancing the competing interests of open justice and confidentiality.

The court papers contain the following statement:

> Mr Justice Gillen noted that there had already been publicity, often misinformed, about the case in the locality where the family live and said that it is important that the full facts are known. He also felt that the workings of the family justice system in the case merited public scrutiny and discussion.

We were free to talk. At last.

By noon, my story was on Northern Ireland radio; by lunchtime, I was being interviewed; by 6 p.m., I was on the television news and by the next day I was in the head-lines again. Carmel found herself in demand for media interviews, too, and despite being a naturally self-effacing person, she was the consummate professional in every appearance, before stepping back to resume her legal practice with her less public cases.

The national papers came, too – the *Daily Mail*, the *Daily Telegraph*, *The Times* and the *Guardian*. The *Mail*'s women's editor, Sue Reid, flew over to meet me in Derry. I seemed to have touched a nerve in the UK consciousness; the fear that the increased powers of the social services and governmental restrictions on personal freedom have quashed the rights of the family. Accompanying editorials spoke of social workers working 'above the law', while one dramatic headline – 'British justice? A family ruined' – lambasted their lack of accountability, and the destruction of parental and human rights.

When a number of Northern Ireland documentary makers got in touch in the days after the news broke, Carmel and I agreed on *Spotlight*. They were one of the teams who had been following my story since my first court appearance and had kept to the reporting restrictions. We respected this.

When we were filming, I mentioned to them that I'd been impressed by Angela Cannings's story. The *Spotlight* team then came up with an idea – would I like to fly over to England to meet Angela and have that meeting recorded? They knew Angela had worked with the BBC before; if they could arrange it, would I go? I was excited at the thought of this. If anyone would understand what I'd been through, she would, I felt.

The minute we met and hugged each other, the flood-gates opened and we talked, wept, laughed and talked some more for hours. The evening flew by. The cameras were irrelevant. We both had so much we wanted to talk about and we kept saying the same things to each other. Angela talked about coming to terms with the fact that her daughter is closer to her estranged husband and lives with him. She warned me it is nearly impossible for a child that has spent its first few years away from you to form a strong bond with its mother. Angela spoke about her need to find some sort of reason for what happened to her, and to try to make some good come out of it. That's why she set up the Angela Cannings Foundation 'to promote more research into the causes of sudden death in infants and children. To encourage open and honest debate about the flaws in the current system.'

Above all, Angela told me she was 'frozen for four years' and I know precisely what she means. You have to survive. People thought I was cold, or hardened, but it wasn't that – it was nature's way of coping. It leaves you very cynical, and very private. You become used to only allowing your emotions free rein behind closed doors. In public, you keep your emotions in check; you remain in control. It's hard to break this pattern. I know I am now much less open, much more wary of people I meet.

In return, I told Angela about what had happened to me. I also told her I was following her lead in writing about my life; she told me she'd found writing very thera-peutic. We promised to keep in touch, and we have.

The public response to my story has been supportive, understanding and generous. I'm getting round to collecting and replying to the letters that have been sent on to me after television appearances and radio interviews, and from magazines and newspapers that have interviewed me. It will take time, but I am more determined than ever to set up a registered charity to co-ordinate information and support for the many families which have been faced with a situation like ours. And we need to ask the question, and ask it urgently – how many children have the Family Courts taken from the mothers who love them, in the name of care?

Leabharlanna Poibli Chathair Bhaile Átha Cliath
Dublin City Public Libraries

ACKNOWLEDGEMENTS

I am especially grateful to my legal team – Carmel, Michael and Ken – whose dedication went beyond the call of duty; to Dr D without whose courage the truth would not have been known; to my friends, Jean, who died tragically in July 2008, and Colum; and to the many people who have helped me along the way.

And lastly, I give thanks to Saint Teresa who has been my comfort during this long journey and will always be with me.